HATCHED

SHARON WALLEN

To chickens everywhere.
You know who you are.

Contents

AUTHOR'S NOTE

The events and insights described in this book played out in my life between April 2004 and May 2005. I first described them in a book I titled *What I've Learned From Chickens*. Finally publishing that book a whole decade later in 2014 required that I swallow a debilitating fear of putting my story out there. Writing it was easy, thinking about other people reading it was torturous. But publish it I did, and that was a miracle.

Once published, however, I disowned it. It was like giving birth to a child, only to put it on a park bench somewhere and wander off, leaving it to make something of its life…or not. In a great continuation of the miracle, however, others stepped forward to nurture my little creation. They wrote reviews, recommended it to friends, or kept a stack next to the cash register in their shops. My son Tom even carried extra copies with him on his travels around the world, passing the book to anyone he thought might benefit from its messages. People like this, these enthusiastic pollinators of ideas, are vital to the blooming of consciousness in our world.

Over the years, stories about the book got back to me. There was a woman who read it aloud to her friend while she was in the hospital receiving cancer treatments. A young mother who read it four times. A man who sent me a photo of his dog-eared copy with notes all over it. The owner of a small company who bought copies for her employees to help bring some of the principles to life in her business. And more than one person ended up with a bunch of chickens of their own. In spite of my cold shoulder, it seems my little book-child has been finding and creating love out in the world.

Recently, I read the book again and although I was able to feel a bit proud that its lessons still resonated, I could sense the fear between the lines. While it did represent my truth, it didn't tell the whole truth. I had withheld critical information because I didn't trust myself to tell it right. I thought I could play small enough to get through life without ever making anyone uncomfortable.

Lots of memoir writers struggle with this. How do we tell our version of the truth when it involves other people? Might it hurt them? What if they get mad at us? It seems simpler to tell half of the story or forget about writing it at all. But, if we're lucky, we are able to rise above the personal narrative to see the larger theme. From that higher perspective, we also see that there are others in the world who are suffering as we have and who would benefit from our truth if responsibly and lovingly told. We grow to understand that helping those people is worth the risk of upsetting a few.

I decided to rewrite the book and so here it is, better I hope and if not better, at least more whole. Three of the names are pseudonyms, but other than that, it is as true as any one person can make a story.

Inspired by all of those steadfast pollinators, I intend to be more nurturing of my book-baby this time, to do more to help it and other books I've learned from to find those who are ready for their messages. You can help, too. When you find a book that moves you, help it to move along—write reviews, share what you've learned, or press a copy upon a heart that needs it.

I can no longer play small, because I'm not small and neither are you. When we help each other to realize this, we will have changed the world.

Many Chicken Blessings to You,
Sharon Wallen
Summer 2021
U.S. Virgin Islands

Prologue

I will always be grateful for what I've learned from observing the natural ways of chickens. Chickens know how to pay close attention to the important things and how to enjoy the deep contentment that comes from forgetting the rest. They take great pride in their work and fully accept their purpose in God's plan. They even know how to die with grace.

The impulsive decision to hatch a bunch of chicken eggs awakened me to many truths about my life. Although acting upon these lessons would bring temporary struggle, this was just what I needed to crack the confining shell of routines and expectations that limited my existence.

As I've told my chicken stories to various friends and family throughout the years, I've noticed that others in the room often lean in to listen. When I speak about how my chickens changed me, eyes begin to sparkle and heads nod as I describe how tense and overwhelmed I used to feel before the chickens came into my life. People say, "I know what you mean. That's how I feel!" They want to know the secret.

Many years have passed since the nine little balls of fluff that are the stars of this story began my transformation, enough time for me to understand that the secret is simple: *We just need to relax into the natural way of things.*

Children are born knowing this, but as we grow "up" in our modern society, we tend to fall into a kind of sleep, slowly closing our eyes, our ears, and our hearts to the gift of divine intelligence that flows all around us. In the course of living, we forget that this gift is part of our true nature.

We need to be reminded—and life certainly does conspire to wake us up in a myriad of challenging ways, doesn't it? But in its kindest form, this remembering comes by way of miracles that gently nudge us awake, and then help us grow "in" to who we really are.

My miracles just happened to have feathers and four-toed dinosaur feet.

LESSON 1:

THE POWER OF YES

A little voice piped up from the seat behind me. "Hey, Mom! Can we hatch 'em?" I was driving home on a misty April evening with my 7-year-old son, Mac, who had a pile of eggs on his lap. This was a request I'd heard several times since we began volunteering to do the chores at an 18th century living-history farm museum, a place where the chickens run free and time breathes deeply.

I answered in the same distracted way I usually did. "No."

That's how any sensible person living in the 21st century with close neighbors, forbidding town ordinances, and barely enough land to pitch a tent would answer.

"Why not?" he said with his typical anything-is-possible optimism. "The hens have a rooster." This was a reference to a delicate talk we'd already had about why we couldn't hatch eggs from the grocery store.

I sighed, gathering my patience for the longer version of No. "They need to be kept warm and we don't have the right equipment. Everything needs to be just right to hatch an egg."

I watched in the rearview mirror as he scrunched his face for a moment. Then he brightened. "Hey, I know what we can do! We can put them under the lamp on the counter!"

"No, we're not going to put them under a lamp. It wouldn't work."

"Can we someday?" he asked.

"We'll see," I said. A grown-up's classic cop-out.

"Does that mean maybe?" A kid's classic reply.

"Maybe."

And the conversation was over. Except a thread had been pulled loose inside of me—things didn't feel tidy. My brow furrowed—*why exactly did I say No?* As I drove along the streets of Bristol, Rhode Island, the charming harbor town we called home, I began to feel haunted by a determined vow I had made as a girl to *not* turn into the kind of mom who says No all the time. It seemed to me then that mothers were quite prone to do that and I had intended to be different. But there I was, a mother myself with another No falling from my lips.

The tomboy I once was shook her finger at me and scowled. She is a powerful, wild creature with briars in her hair, a bandage on her elbow, and a flush of poison ivy on her shin. She intimidates me. She has not yet learned that there is a bunch of stuff she cannot do and so she can still do anything. She jumps onto the bare backs of horses that do not belong to her and rides without permission. She stares down the boys who don't play fair and isn't afraid to punch them if she needs to. She can probably even fly. And she wanted to hatch some eggs.

But seriously, I said to the girl within, *of course, we're not going to hatch eggs. What would we do with the chickens? We don't have any room!* My tomboy folded her arms and turned her head away, disgusted. *You are no fun,* she said. *Where has your sense of adventure gone?*

Where indeed? I wondered. The question lingered for a few minutes and then faded away as I pulled into the driveway, distracted immediately by the countless tasks I needed to perform, like boiling water for pasta, emptying the dishwasher, getting everyone started on their homework, and taking out the trash.

The next morning, we ate the farm eggs for breakfast.

The following week at the farm, I moved the sheep from the pasture into their pen and carried buckets of water to the oxen as Mac ran around with Belle, the farm beagle, searching through the hay for eggs. He had 13 eggs in a bucket by the time we were ready to leave. David, the manager of Coggeshall Farm, walked over with an empty basket to make it easier for us to take them home. He was dressed as an 18th century farmer in hand-sewn and patched trousers, a simple cloth shirt, a primitive felt hat, and shoes he actually made himself. The authentic clothing isn't merely his farm museum costume; it is his preference, whether on the farm or off. He has the appearance and gentle, wise demeanor of Abe Lincoln. When he talks, I listen.

"You know…" he said with his characteristic pause; he makes me wait for the rest, which might be why I listen better. "I have an incubator if you'd ever like to hatch any eggs."

Before I could stop her, the neglected 12-year-old in me leapt up from my belly and socked me in the arm. "Yes! Let's do it," she said before I could get a word in edgewise. I was apparently possessed because those very words came out of my mouth. It was a done deal.

I waited for the familiar crush I used to feel whenever anything was added to the enormous pile of duties I already didn't have enough time for, but instead of that vague throwuppy feeling, I experienced something else. In that instant of enthusiastic Yes!, decades of tension left my body. I was in the here and now, like a child, completely absorbed in the brilliant new adventure of hatching eggs. All the cells in my body slurped thirstily as this feeling, this fresh, clean rain washed my muddy tension away.

Within minutes, David was handing me a flimsy Styrofoam incubator and I was asking him how to use it as Mac bounced around in glee. The eggs had already become our babies instead of a quiche.

On the drive home through the long afternoon shadows, I was filled with an excited peace. Mac sat with the eggs on his lap and we chatted happily about their potential as chicks instead of shiny orange yolks, wiggling on a plate. Even Shanti, our regal black standard poodle, seemed to sit taller next to Mac in the back seat. My typically relentless thinking, thinking, thinking about logistical worries was replaced by an absolute focus on that moment of co-creation with my boy, the hens, their rooster, and Something Greater that I did not yet have a name for.

Looking back, I can clearly see that transcendent moment of Yes, that moment when the layers of fear and doubt inside of me began to be replaced with light and ease. Like many women I know, my life had become overloaded. With a blended family of six to manage, day-to-day demands had worn away the courage, spontaneity, and joy I'd embodied as a girl. I felt that if I didn't control everything, we would spin off into space. It felt as if saying No and thinking of reasons Why Not were the fences in our life that kept us safe.

After being stuck in the habit of the reflexive No for years, saying Yes to chickens was an ecstatic coloring outside of the lines. It didn't make sense; it was silly and foolish and weird. But in spite of that (or maybe because of it), a bubbling fountain of joy had welled up, turning my weary inner frown into a jubilant smile. In that one affirming breath, I took a chip out of the protective layers I had built around my authentic self—the self I was born to be.

From my new perspective, I can ask *What happened to the real me?* As a child, I was full of wonder about the world.

I saw it as it truly is: a place of infinite, magical possibilities, a place where I could make anything happen. Like most children raised before the age of virtual gaming and countless streaming options, I used my imagination constantly and played outside every spare moment. I got dirty. I fell down, brushed myself off, and got going again. I came home delighted and tired. My mother usually didn't know where I was for hours at a time—and no one ever thought to call the authorities. I was free to experience nature and my world with wild abandon.

This capacity for wonder is innate in most children when they are left to themselves; it is our birthright. Watch a young child play. Notice the sense of abundance and possibility, the complete lack of conceptualized fear. As we grow into adulthood, however, we start to see the world as a smaller, more limiting place. In school, we are told to sit still, stay in line, and be quiet—all variations of No that make the teacher's job not just easier but possible. In the media, we are fed a constant stream of stories and images that trigger fear. Our learned desire to stay safe and comfortable becomes a shell that retards our growth—in fact, most of us don't grow at all; we shrink. By the time we're thirty, we have absorbed far more reasons to say No than to say Yes.

Of course, the word No has its place. No is an amazing discovery for a new parent—a remote control device. When the child reaches for the cat's tail or a hot radiator or a glass vase, we can shout No! from across the room and the crisis is averted. I think we first start saying No to our children for very good reasons.

But as children grow older, their requests require more thought. "Mom, can we carve our Halloween pumpkins now?" they might have asked me just as I'd put on my boots to go rake the lawn. Thinking about their request required time and energy. If I did bother to think about it at all, my thoughts might have gone like this: *It's four o'clock and I need to rake those leaves now. If I don't, then I'll have to do it tomorrow and there's a chance it will rain before then and the leaves will get too heavy...*and so on. It was too much to figure out most of the time and the default became No simply because it was easier. What if the default were Yes? "Yes, that's a great idea!" or even, "Yes, but I need your help raking for an hour first." There are so many creative options as to how and when we get things done, but they all flow from Yes. Nothing creative ever came from No.

Of course, as a parent, I still said No. The answer to "Can I eat all of my Halloween candy?" was still usually No, but I tried to be more present for the question and answer more consciously. That awareness makes all the difference, for I also tried saying, "Yes! Eat as much as you want." And when I did, the delicious surprise of the Yes! was so sweet that only a moderate amount of candy was actually consumed. Apparently, their souls needed Yes! more than their tongues needed sugar.

There are many ways to practice saying Yes. I once had a dear friend named Caryn who taught me about something she called Hoobly Shoobly. Hoobly Shoobly is an attitude, a state of mind; it is all about Yes. Caryn and I met while working in Bar Harbor, Maine, during the summer between my freshman and sophomore years in college. We found each other at the YWCA where we were both staying and soon discovered that we shared a love of exploration and sunrises.

"Let's Hoobly Shoobly," she'd say in her soft Maryland accent and off we'd go. We'd jump in her car and start driving through the lush green of Mount Desert Island in whatever direction called to us. If either one of us saw a side road that beckoned, we'd take it, even if it meant making a sudden screeching turn. We laughed until our cheeks hurt and stuck our heads out the window to view the bright blue sky. The expansive spirit of Yes guided us to some spectacular sights and profound encounters with people. When we got lost (and we always did), we let our intuition guide us back to something familiar and it never let us down. That experience of turning off our minds and placing all of our trust in our hearts created a giddy sensation of freedom and bliss. Sometimes we celebrated our Hoobly spirit at the top of Cadillac Mountain, where we'd share a cup of cheap champagne as we watched the sunrise, delighting in the fact that we were the first people in the continental United States to feel the sun on our faces that day.

When I first took on my roles as mom, stepmom, and wife, I had abundant Hoobly energy. I made creative meals that we ate by candlelight on the Royal Doulton china my grandmother had given me as a wedding gift. I refused to succumb to the norm of getting a big TV with cable, so our viewing was limited to what we could see on a 12-inch screen with a rabbit ear antenna. Without television to distract us, we found the time to play games, talk, and go for walks. A big treat was when I'd bring a big box home from the appliance store and put it in the middle of the living room for the kids (and me) to make forts out of. We had fun. *I* was fun.

But by the time the eggs were carefully placed on Mac's lap that spring evening, I had become significantly less jolly. There were many reasons for this. On a head level, the writing deadlines I faced to earn our living and the challenge of managing the crazy logistics of our busy family had thrown me into a state of anxious overwhelm.

On a physical level, I was overdoing, doing, doing. I couldn't seem to get ahead of all the household tasks—there was the fancy china to wash and bills to pay and bathrooms to clean. Every time I turned around, a forgotten load of laundry had turned mildewy in the washing machine and my car's "check engine" light was on. Like many, my to-do list was too long, so I did what most of us do: I buckled down and worked even harder to try to somehow beat the odds. I chased the list compulsively, as if our lives depended upon it. I honestly thought they did.

On a heart level, I felt like I was on my own. My husband, Paul, wasn't very good at helping with all I thought I had to do (I can see now how much of that was optional), and I had given up asking him to. It was easier to just do everything myself. This unconscious decision to make myself a lonely martyr rather than be honest about what I needed was at the core of much of the heartbreak that came our way.

This was my second marriage and, like most, it had its ups and downs. During our first five years, Paul and I had laughed and loved in great abundance. We brought our respective children together, created a loving home, and welcomed Mac into the world. As my feelings of overwhelm had grown, though, so did my resentment toward Paul.

At first, this happened in nearly imperceptible ways that I could easily ignore by making myself busier. But then came the blows of 2001—first my darling father lost his fight with lung cancer, then a beloved dog and cat died within two weeks of each other, and then came the collective horror of the attack on the World Trade Center in New York City that September.

In the midst of all this sorrow, on a beautiful late summer afternoon, I was home alone just puttering around when I stumbled upon evidence that Paul was having an affair. This was a horrifying shock, but I managed to absorb it quickly with the help of my dear friend Kendra who rushed to help me when I called. She found me frantically pacing and ranting, but somehow managed to quiet me down.

"Come sit," she said moving me toward the cozy nook in the kitchen where we always had our best chats.

I followed and sat in the comfy chair across from her.

"How are you feeling?" she asked.

Kendra was the feeling one of us and had more than once tried to open my mind to the idea that perhaps I needed to feel more. This always made me uncomfortable. To her point, I usually didn't know how to answer when she wanted to know how I was feeling, but on that day it was easy. "I feel fucking furious. Murderous even."

"What do you want to do?"

"Throw all of his crap out onto the street," I sputtered.

"Do you love him?"

Ahhhhhrrr! My brain felt like it would explode. I certainly didn't *want* to love him.

She waited patiently; she who knew my whole story with all of its sordid bits. She who knew about my guilt over my own past transgressions when it came to fidelity in my previous marriage; she who knew that I was worth loving even so.

I started to cry, covering my face with my hands to try to hold in the too-much feeling that was now oozing out. "Yes," I blubbered. "I do love him."

When I quieted, she asked, "So what are you *going* to do?"

"I'm going to try to make it work somehow."

I did try. Paul did, too. He ended things with *her*

immediately and in the following months held steady during my occasional episodes of hurt and anger as I struggled mightily to reconcile the truth of his affair with my previous precious conviction that this would *never* happen to *us*.

But it did happen. To us.

I decided to forgive and forget for the family's sake. But looking back I see that I was faking it. This was just more emotional dishonesty and hiding of the truth from myself. I didn't really forgive him and I certainly didn't forget. I just noodled on the situation with the conscious part of my brain until I found a way to make it not his fault. A weird sort of logic dictated that this was the only way I could stay with him—and stay out of jail—for if I were to assign him responsibility for his actions, the beast that was my righteous anger would certainly erupt and probably kill him.

Instead, I made him a victim of the other woman's manipulations. I made him the victim of her narcissistic personality disorder. But mostly, I made him a victim of my being so obsessed with doing and controlling everything that I had forgotten how to be a compassionate partner. I also decided that because I had hurt someone else in exactly this same way, this was just karma playing out—I deserved it. I can see now that trying to take all responsibility upon myself was just another way of controlling things and of minimizing Paul.

However flawed, my approach seemed to work for a while and we had several relatively happy months. Unfortunately, while my conscious mind was busy with all that excuse making, the unconscious part was letting furious thoughts run endless laps around my brain until I was a cauldron of resentment and bitterness on the inside with a cheery smile plastered on the outside. None of this felt like a choice—it was just what my heartbroken system did to survive.

The problem with making him a victim was that I lost respect for him. In spite of the hours of therapy, in spite of reading the books on relationships, in spite of wearing the phony smile, a flame had gone out inside of me. I discovered, too late, that love and respect are intricately bound.

It was all too much to deal with at the time, so although I went through the motions and did all the outward-facing things that would continue to make me appear success-ful—including pretending (even to myself) that I was hap-pily married—the candles went out, the television went on, and I succumbed to the false serenity offered by the next bottle of wine.

That is my truth about what happened to me.

Meanwhile, my husband went through his own contor-tions to recommit to our family, enduring hours of therapy and relationship books right alongside me. Perhaps with enough time, these efforts would have borne the healing fruits of trust and respect and we could have found love again, but instead of drowning his sorrows in wine like me, he secretly became overly fascinated with the world of online porn. This new brand of porn was ascending in its power to destroy lives during precisely this time as broad-band internet was quickly replacing slow dial-up modems.

With an endless supply of perfect images or any odd fetish one could imagine, with the power to instantly create a fantasy or even an actual virtual relationship upon the click of a button, the lure of internet porn is impossible for many to resist. And while it is not yet technically classified as an addiction, maybe it should be.

When we fall in love, we all enjoy a cocktail of blissful chemicals produced by our brain's hypothalamus that make us feel euphoric and energetic. We may be so giddy under the influence of natural love hormones like dopamine and norepinephrine that we lose our appetite and become too excited to sleep. For many who are consumed by it, online porn is not necessarily a source of physical sexual release; it is an addiction to these feelings of bliss that are produced by our bodies under the influence of love, whether real or imagined.

Here's what no one knew back then: As internet porn users exercise their power to click through stimulating and infinitely novel images on-line, the intoxicating love drugs reward the behavior, eventually lulling them into a flow state that makes the rest of life disappear. A real life—a real wife—cannot compete with the delicious felt experience of having an imaginary perfect new lover every minute or two.

That is my truth about what happened to my husband.

Needless to say, this was not very beneficial to our healing process as a couple. So off we went to more therapy for this new problem. Unfortunately, he continued to insist upon his right to continue the behavior. "It's not hurting anyone," he said. "I should be able to look at whatever I want during my private time."

During those early years of the internet, therapists didn't yet have the tools to understand the real threat of on-line porn; they lumped it together with the relatively harmless old-fashioned activity of looking at girly magazines. I honestly wished it was that simple and I tried to view it that way. But the toll it took upon Paul and our marriage was devastating. He stopped sleeping regular hours so he could spend more time in front of his computer. He lost his ability to focus on his work, on his children, on the tasks required to run a household. I had to take on more work to make up for his lost income, which only increased my feelings of overwhelm. And as my resentment grew, so did his need to escape his own feelings of guilt and unworthiness as he failed to participate in our life together.

We fell into a downward spiral. Without the language of addiction to support our understanding and get help for the problem, he spent more and more time chasing his high and I simply gave up trying to stop him, deciding instead that the path to peace was to pretend for the kids' sake that everything was fine. So I did what I'd always done—I got busy and tried to simply ignore the problem. The trouble with that strategy was that I also increasingly ignored him.

That is my truth about what happened to our marriage.

But on the day we brought the eggs home I hadn't said Yes to these truths yet. They were still safely tucked away in some inner vault where I stored such things. I imagine it had a label on it that said something like: *WARNING: Opening this door may result in the complete annihilation of all you hold dear!* For extra security, the vault was protected by a swirling force field that hummed with all of the busy, mind-numbing activities I had created for myself. Oblivious to the ways I had confined my life to maintaining the status quo, I tucked myself within a shell of imagined security, and ignored the truths that could set me free.

And yet, on that soft April night as Mac and I lifted those thirteen perfect eggs out of the car and carried them into the house, I felt a shift. It was the subtle warmth of a Hoobly sun rising—the power of Yes was once again being unleashed in my life.

LESSON 2:

WAIT FOR 21 DAYS

L ater that same evening, after dinner was over and the homework was in progress, I found myself alone with the eggs for a few minutes. I looked down at them, still waiting in their basket. Suddenly, it was as if I'd never really seen an egg before. I held one in my hand, admiring its shape, slowly running my fingers over the smooth surface. It was perfect. Then I picked up the cheap Styrofoam incubator with its scratched plastic window and its jiggly wire for adjusting the temperature. I seriously doubted the contraption's ability to play mother hen to my eggs.

You see, God gave the hen everything she needs to succeed when it comes to hatching eggs. She carries with her the perfect environment, all the right instincts, and the patience of a saint. Left to herself, a chicken with the urge to brood creates a nest somewhere off the beaten path where neither fox nor farmer can find her and lays an egg every day or so for a couple of weeks until she has a nest full. Only then does she settle herself onto the eggs and hunker down for the long wait.

The first miracle of fertilized eggs is that they can remain viable for more than two weeks while waiting for their mother hen to feel the urge to sit. They don't start to develop into chicks until they reach 55% humidity and the critical temperature of 99 degrees Fahrenheit, the exact conditions that you would find if you took measurements under the downy breast of a broody hen. Once the hen sits, she spreads herself out over her eggs and gets very still. Then she sits and sits—and sits—and sits some more—for 21 whole days. On the 21st day, even though her eggs have been laid over the course of two weeks, they all hatch within 24 hours of each other. This let's-all-hatch-together instinct is critical to the success of the species because, unlike most birds whose chicks are born naked, blind, and helpless, chickens have independent hatchlings who are protected by feathers and immediately able to feed themselves. Once they hatch, they start wandering off and it would be an impossible job for the hen to watch over the first hatchlings while still sitting on the rest of the eggs.

Nature sure has everything all figured out, but I, being featherless, did not. All I had was a dirty plastic box with a hard wire bottom and a squeaky lid. I lifted the incubator off the table and placed it on the floor—so it couldn't possibly fall—under the sideboard table in an out-of-the-way corner of the dining room. I plugged it in and waited. The thermometer rose to 102 degrees. I tried to turn it down with the jiggly wire thing and it fell to 95 degrees. For over an hour, I jiggled the wire and watched the temperature bounce all around the ideal of 99 degrees without ever landing there.

After getting ready for bed, the kids all gathered around and we made the joint decision to put the eggs in and hope for the best.

I woke up early the next morning eager to check on the eggs. With an excited Shanti scampering by my side, I hurried down the stairs and through the house in the dim predawn light. I switched on the lamp that sat on the table above the incubator and squatted down. The Styrofoam lid screeched as I opened it and warm, moist air rose to meet my face—it smelled like life. The thermometer read close to, but not quite, 99 degrees. I wiggled the wire a tiny bit and sighed, still hopeful but very unsure that the incubator was doing its job.

David the farmer had told me that the eggs in an incubator need to be turned and shuffled at least three times a day to simulate the action of a hen moving the eggs around with her feet. I marked each egg with an X so I could see which side was which. Then I moved them around carefully in spite of Shanti's inquisitive nose—placing those on the inside of the "nest" on the outside and moving those on the outside to the inside. I marveled at the way the eggs fit into my hand, smooth and warm—substantial yet delicate. Once they were in their new positions, I turned them over, working quickly so I could close the cover before they got too cold.

I paused for a moment after the closing the lid, curious about the peace I felt inside. If you had asked me before I said Yes! to chickens if I would be willing to turn and rotate eggs three times a day for 21 days, I might have slapped you. But performing this simple task (the task of a hen's feet!) expanded my heart and focused my mind in ways that were unfamiliar and lovely. I knew there were many things I would do that day that were much more important to my family, but that one small duty felt most important to my own spirit. The blessings that sprouted inside of me were immediate and abundant. I didn't understand why this was so, but I was grateful.

The next week found us back at the farm right on schedule. Belle the beagle howled her greeting and ran around in excited circles when she saw us coming. David, who was walking up from the pasture, just waved.

"Hullo," he said when he got closer. "Did you get your eggs started?"

"I hope so," I said. "It took a while for the incubator to settle down after we put them in."

"It would have been a good idea to wait until it settled *before* you put them in," he said calmly.

My heart flopped over in my chest. "Do you think we killed them?" I was fighting panic.

"Well," he paused to carefully consider my question. "They weren't really alive yet, were they? Not much difference between that and hard boiling them." He looked down at me with his eyes sparkling.

I thought about this. "No, I guess not."

"Take some more eggs today and put them in with the others. See what happens."

As we fed the sheep, Mac discovered five more eggs tucked into the hay in a corner of the manger. He lit up with excitement and gathered them into his shirt with care. We brought them home, marked them with an "O" to distinguish them from the first batch and added them to the pile in the incubator. These new eggs would be a week behind the others who, with luck, had started developing the moment they first felt the warmth of the incubator.

We headed over to the calendar beside the kitchen door and Mac marked off another day. This was Day 7 for the first batch of eggs and Day 21—their due date—was circled in red. Then he drew a green star around Day 28, which would be the due date for the second batch. He looked up at me when he was done, smiling his newest smile, which changed daily with every baby tooth that fell out and big one that grew in. He was happy because we had five more eggs than we had before, and when you are seven, more is always better. I was happy because I had a backup plan, some insurance against total failure. I was in control again.

I included the eggs with an "O" in the egg shuffling process several times a day. Sometimes I did it alone, and other times I watched as Mac handled the eggs with great concentration and gentleness—I was totally captivated by his sweetness. Every moment spent with the eggs, in fact, filled me with a new form of joy. I never hurried through the job and it never became humdrum; I was simply and completely absorbed in the task. Given how swamped I felt at the time, it was a miracle that caring for the eggs never felt like a burden. They were always on my mind as a pleasant distraction, providing a sense of purpose each day, something outside of the routine, something outside of myself, and I was immensely interested.

I find it fascinating that the 21 days it takes for a chick to develop and hatch is the same amount of time it takes for the synapses in the human brain to stabilize when we introduce a change to our routine. While caring for the eggs, I was actually creating new habits of positive thought and emotion. As I waited, my heart grew and the inexplicable love I felt for the unborn chicks began to melt the crust of resentment and control I had allowed to build up over the years.

In my efforts to take care of everyone, I had developed fear-based habits of planning that I thought were necessary to get through each week. If I didn't know where every member of the family was, what they needed, where they were going, and how they were going to get there, then how would we all survive? The mental effort of staying eight steps ahead of every eventuality was exhausting, but I did it without knowing there was a choice.

Our society nurtures an illusion that we can control our lives and holds being "in control" as a virtue. From the time we are very small, we are rewarded for doing what we are told, staying quiet, and putting our crayons back in their box. It doesn't take long for us to notice that when we lose control and get a bit messy, the people we love and depend upon get upset. Schools reinforce this belief by teaching us that we can control our destiny by just showing up and turning in our homework; doing so results in an automatic progression through the grades until we pop out the other end of the pre-programmed chute. Most of us emerge right on schedule, meeting expectations and clinging to the illusion of control like a thumb-sucking toddler clings to her blankie. And control does seem to work for a while; if we keep all of our balls in the air and display lots of productive busyness, we are considered successful.

Western culture even seems to foster a certain competitiveness to see who can claim the title of "Busiest" or "Hardest Working" and it is easy to get caught up in this game. Things get more complicated, however, as time goes on and the list of things we need to control grows. It is easy to get lost in controlling our primary relationship, our children, our household, our emotions, our pets, our careers, our weight, our friends, our parents, our automobiles, and the height of the grass that grows in the yard. We even watch the meteorologists obsessively, hoping for some sense of certainty about the weather. Taking all of this on as our personal responsibility is draining and it is no wonder so many of us are running on empty and losing our light as we white-knuckle our way through life.

To my astonishment, caring for the eggs never made it to my to-do list. This is remarkable because my list was my life. It grew very long each week as I crossed things off and added new tasks. I tracked the status of all the things I felt I needed to accomplish to keep our family running—if something wasn't on the list, it probably wasn't going to happen. How then did the eggs get turned at least three times every single day? Why didn't I forget about them? It's not like they were crying or fussing to demand my attention. They just sat there silently, waiting.

The answer, I think, is that the eggs spoke to me through my heart and I was drawn to them when they needed me by an intuitive connection that is not easily explained by the mortal brain. To my higher-level intelligence, the eggs *mattered*, whereas calling to arrange our checkups at the dentist did not. The stuff that was important to my head required writing down; the stuff that was important to my heart called to me, sang to me, and shimmered with such a beautiful light that it was impossible to forget.

Simply waiting for the chicks that were to come pulled me into the natural flow of life. This shift, while subtle at first, changed me. Bit by conscious bit, I relinquished my role as Master Controller of All Family Sustenance and Destiny. And, miraculously, life went on in our household.

Another aspect of control that began to shift for me was my need to know how something would turn out before beginning it. When I held the deluded notion that I was in control of my life, I didn't feel safe stepping onto a path unless I could see exactly where it would lead. This need for certainty and foreknowledge caused a sort of paralysis—my need to *know* the outcome before taking action often meant taking no action at all.

Saying Yes! to the chickens taught me that true freedom and abundance come only when I find the courage to follow my higher guidance *without* knowing for sure where it will lead. I honestly had no idea what we would do with the chicks once they hatched and, quite uncharacteristically, I didn't spend any time worrying about it. I just waited like a good mother hen, completely focused on the task at hand, turning my eggs every day, loving the moment, and trusting that I would have what I needed at each step of the way.

Profound blessings have come to me from this way of living. I've grown to trust the infinite potential contained in that uncertain first step—it's where the angels live, and if we can meet them there, they will always come to take us flying with them.

One morning, exactly three weeks after we brought the first batch of eggs home, the angels woke me extra early. Not yet fully awake, I slipped out of bed and moved through the stillness, listening to the steam radiators whisper their first warming sighs. I made my way to the dining room, switched on the lamp, and squatted down next to the eggs. As usual, I lifted the lid to the incubator and reached for one of the eggs to turn it. My hand stopped midway and a flutter of excitement ran through my whole body. The joyful wait was over.

The egg had a hole in it.

THE VALUE OF THE STRUGGLE

I peered through the hole in the egg and saw dark, wet feathers and a tiny body breathing very hard. I stared in awe. Then I remembered that I was letting all the heat out of the incubator and closed the lid quickly. My newfound willingness to go with the flow vanished as my mind sprang into high alert, searching for things to do and worry about. I leaned in closer to try to look through the little plastic window. The chick wasn't doing anything. Maybe it needed help. It might die! I needed it to live now as much as I needed my own heart to beat.

I ran to the computer and pulled up the Google search page. I typed in "Hatching chicken eggs" and waited while over 895,000 results came back. I clicked on one and quickly scrolled down to learn about the moment of hatching. Here is what it said:

"A little hole or crack in the shell will be the first indicator of hatching. The process may take a day or more. Be patient. You may be tempted to help the chick cast off the shell but resist the urge. Rule one: Don't touch the eggs during the hatching process. The chicks have to do it all by themselves or they will die."

I sat there in the light of the computer monitor, blinking. So, I was to do nothing? *Nothing?! Hmmm*, I thought, *that couldn't be right. There must be some helpful action I could take.* The words on the screen wavered at me: "Don't touch…The chicks have to do it all by themselves." I let the words settle in and felt the weight of needing to help leave my body. There was nothing for me to do. No action was required. The chick would make its way out of its shell—or not. And if it did make it out, it would be stronger for having struggled, ready to tackle the job of surviving out in the big world. My only job was to sit back and accept whatever happened to the little chick I already loved.

Has there ever been a harder assignment in the history of humanity?

I stood slowly, wary of the eerie calm I felt; there was a fragility about it that made me want to tiptoe. I went back to the incubator and sat on the floor so I could watch through the little window. The chick's body pulsed rapidly as it breathed and then it was very still. Too still. For several long moments, nothing happened at all and I wondered: *how could it possibly hurt if I just picked a little chunk of shell off its back?* The pressure grew in my belly until I thought I'd puke—*"DO SOMETHING!"* it screamed. But I just waited until the pressure left; I was committed to letting this chick find its own way.

As I watched that first little chick labor, pecking mightily for short bursts and then becoming still again, I thought about how often my efforts to "help" may have robbed someone of an experience they needed to go through. Was it possible that I should step back more often and trust that the people I love would get more of what they needed by struggling through things themselves? It began to dawn on me that helping was sometimes selfish on my part, for I often jumped in to help because watching someone struggle made *me* uncomfortable. If Mac got frustrated while trying to tie his shoes, I would lean down to help, which almost always ended in me tying them for him. The benefits to me were twofold: 1) I didn't have to witness his struggle, and 2) it was faster so we could get on with our busy day. How much more valuable would it have been if I had taken a step back and given him the space and time he needed to do it himself?

After the chicks reminded me of the value of struggle, I tried to be more of a watchful guardian to my children than the helpful enabler I had been. Out on the playground, I learned to hang back if Mac got into a disagreement with another child.

"Why didn't you tell him to give me the swing back, Mommy?" he asked later, confused and a bit hurt by my lack of involvement.

"Because then you wouldn't have learned how to handle it yourself," I replied.

At this, he brightened; it made intrinsic sense to him, which reaffirmed its rightness to me. Children know what they need and they are hugely resourceful if we can stand by patiently while they struggle to figure something out. This is one of the most important gifts we can give them.

In addition to being good for Mac, my lesson about struggle came just in time to give my 16-year-old son, Tom, the extra freedom he needed to get himself into jams—and then to get out again—on his own. He excitedly took over my old car as soon as he had his license, but learned over time what it meant to also have complete responsibility for all of the expenses that went with it. Tom struggled through many adventures with that car and nearly every penny he earned went into it. When I heard about some of his snafus, I swallowed hard and told him, "You'll figure something out." And he always did. He also lost his romanticized notion of car ownership much earlier than most, coming to me before he left for college to say, "Hey Mom, will you please take the car back? It's a huge pain in the ass and I don't want to have it at school." I can't think of a better way to teach the foundational lesson that with freedom comes responsibility.

The teenage years are all about getting out of the protective shell of childhood. If we make life too easy for them, we rob our children of the experiences they need to survive in this world. Teenagers intuitively know this, which is why they push their helpful, overly-controlling parents away so roughly sometimes. Rather than let this reaction strain our relationship with our kids, we parents would do better to celebrate it—for when we demonstrate our trust in them, they don't need to push away so hard.

As I've shared this lesson with friends and clients, they sometimes take in a sharp breath and whisper the unspeakable, "But if I don't ground her for the rest of high school, she might die." While there is always that small chance—surviving our teenage years is never guaranteed—fully living the *remainder* of our years depends upon our ability to figure things out for ourselves. It's the difference between successful independence and a life of chronic dependence, depression, and dis-ease.

Sadly, the overly protective mindset of many modern parents has led to an epidemic of young people who suffer from a learned helplessness that breeds anxiety, which can lead to subsequent addiction as they seek substances that temporarily relieve it. Of course, we are all well-intended, but the truth is that we often overreact due to irrational fears that greatly inflate the actual risk to our child. Most teenage struggles are not even close to being in the life-or-death category and all we are really saving them from are the struggles required for their learning and healthy growth. Finding the courage to love them enough to let them fail and be uncomfortable now and then, will help them learn how powerfully resilient they actually are.

Letting my own oldest chick struggle paid off. Tom gave

me a birthday card just before he went off to college. "Dear Mom," it said, "thank you for letting me live this last year of my childhood *my* way." There were tears of joy in my eyes as I realized that by letting him struggle, I had given my son the gift of confidence and independence as he pushed the last bit of his child's shell away.

What about my own struggles? How had they shaped me?

I thought back to my college days when I didn't have enough money for food. I remember feeling resentful whenever a friend would get a check from her dad in the mail on Saturdays. Self-pity would sometimes sweep me up in its arms and I let myself wallow in it. *"Where's my check?"* I'd wail silently. *"How come my dad doesn't send me a check?"* This is in spite of the fact that he was already generously paying for *all* of my tuition and rent. When I stopped blubbering, I got back to doing what I had to do to earn money for food. I found jobs that fit around my class schedule and, instead of indulging in the expensive cafeteria plan, I learned how to prepare simple and inexpensive meals that were extremely healthy. I felt a deep pride that I was able to stay on the Dean's List in my engineering courses and still find time to work, cook, walk to the grocery store, and schlep those heavy bags home.

The struggle of that particular challenge taught me how to take care of myself—a lesson that has led to a life of unfettered freedom and personal choice that is unlike that of some of my well-cared-for-by-daddy friends. I learned to step up to the plate and swing and swing and swing until I got a hit. I developed discipline, perseverance, and the confidence that I would always find my way. This level of trust in one's own abilities cannot be bought; it must be earned through struggle and accomplishment. There is no other way.

It occurred to me as I thought about all of this that I had stopped actively engaging in the struggles of my adult life. Not because I had been victorious in growing through the discomfort I experienced, but because I had succeeded in ignoring it. I had shut down, given up. I was hiding in my protective shell and, although I was not at all sure I was ready to come out, perhaps it was time to consider making my first crack.

Unlike me, that first little chick broke free of its shell on the 21st day, and then another chick and another. Mac stayed home from school and, with Shanti proudly standing guard, we watched as eight chicks —pecked, kicked, and squirmed heroically—to break free of their shells. One at a time, each little wet body collapsed on the wire floor of the warm incubator and lay there panting until it recovered from the ordeal of entering this world. Once the chick was fluffy and dry, we gently lifted it out and placed it in a cardboard box with a warm desk lamp hanging over the side that we'd set up on the dining room table.

By evening, ten eggs remained in the incubator, five that should have hatched with the others and five that still had a week to go. Eight little puff balls peeped softly and scurried about in their new cardboard home. The chicks seemed to particularly enjoy pooping in their water dish and tossing the grainy chick mash all around until, eventually, they all fell asleep in a heap.

We marveled at their antics together until, one by one, the kids each went off to bed. Later, I returned to the chicks and stood alone in the quiet for a long time, feeling deeply content as I watched them breathe.

LESSON 4:

ATTITUDE IS EVERYTHING

One week to the day after the first chicks hatched, I came downstairs in the morning to find one lonely chick standing in the incubator, the sole hatchee of the second batch of eggs. It just stood there blinking in the strange surroundings, probably instinctively knowing that this Styrofoam world was not what nature had intended for it. I opened the lid and gathered the new life into my hands. I brought it up to my face and we looked at each other for a moment, then I put it with the other chicks in the box on the dining room table.

Immediately, the older chicks rushed over as a pack and began viciously pecking at it. "STOP IT!!" I screeched, snatching the new chick out of there as fast as I could. I held it against my chest, both of our hearts pounding fast.

Now what was I going to do? The older chicks were already nearly twice the size of this little one after only a week of growing and, apparently, putting them together wasn't going to work. I slumped into a chair to think about this while the little chick snuggled into the nest my hand made against my chest. This made me swoon—a mother hen was I.

After enjoying the tender moment, I got back to thinking about my problem. I had one chick that wasn't accepted by the others. I certainly hadn't counted on that. While a certain amount of struggle is a good thing for a young chick, I couldn't allow it to be murdered! I also couldn't carry it around with me all day, so I put the lone chick back in the incubator and went in search of another box. Soon this newest ball of fluff had a separate habitat all its own. My thirteen-year-old stepson, Patrick, named this chick Abe, and even though we later discovered that Abe was a girl, Abe she remained.

Within the next few days, it became clear that the eight older chicks were quickly outgrowing their box on the dining room table and would need a larger space. It was too soon to put them outside, so Mac and I headed off to the appliance store and came home with a giant dishwasher box. We put it on the floor, cut the sides down a bit, and layered it with a thick pad of newspaper. Mac added a bowl of food and I decided to try something new to see if I could stop the chicks from pooping in their water. I filled a small cup with water and placed a shallow saucer over it. Then I turned the whole thing upside-down. Just as I hoped, a small amount of water seeped out from under the bowl and filled the saucer. As the chicks drank, more water was released. I put this contraption up on another inverted bowl to make it the same height as the chick's heads. After hanging a lamp over the edge, the new home was complete and it was time to move the birds into it.

On a hunch, I took little Abe and put her in first. Mac and I watched her scamper around by herself for twenty minutes or so. Then we decided to add the other chicks one at a time. As Mac set the second chick into the box, Abe ran over and pecked it once on the beak. *Bonk*. For some reason, this caused the second chick to freeze in place. It didn't move for several long moments and when it did, Abe pecked it on the beak again. *Bonk*. I added another chick and the same thing happened. Whenever they moved, Abe pecked them on the beak and froze them again. We added another and another until they were all in the box together, and Abe pecked each in turn as it was added. *Bonk. Bonk. Bonk*. Abe couldn't keep up with them all after a while and they started moving around. Some went over to eat and Abe ran over and chased them off. Abe ate first and only then were the others allowed to eat. Little Abe was still half the size of the older chicks, but she clearly ruled the roost. And she was never the victim again. Within an hour, all of the chicks were running around together as one flock.

What happened? How had Abe gone from being the victim to being the boss within a few days? Clearly, Abe decided that the new box belonged to her during the twenty minutes she was alone in there and she was defending her space. It reminded me of the old saying: It's not the size of the dog in a fight that matters; it's the size of the fight in the dog.

Little Abe had stood her ground in a big way.

In this case, the chick benefited from a lack of information—specifically, a lack of memory of the past and a lack of worry about the future. She didn't know she was smaller than the others. She didn't remember that they had attacked her just a few days earlier, so she was not paralyzed with fear that they would attack her again. The only thing she knew was that each bird was entering *her* space and needed to be dealt with. She had no limiting beliefs about her abilities or her rights; she only had chutzpah and attitude.

Little Abe was lucky to be born a chicken. We humans, on the other hand, get bound up in false beliefs about ourselves; we let others tell us who we are and how we are supposed to fit into our groups, our families, and into society as a whole. We buy into collective beliefs about how we should age, how our children are supposed to turn out, how hard it needs to be to earn a living, and what a marriage is supposed to look like.

As I watched Abe spontaneously create new rules for her life, I felt pecked at by feelings of disappointment and apprehension about how I was living mine. I started thinking it would be nice to have a reset button like little Abe.

We actually all do have a reset button, but we tend to stop using it once we become adults and get set in our ways. Like many, I had accepted the bullshit story we're told about what being an adult is supposed to look like and had willingly traded the freedom of living my biggest and best life ⌐fining creature comforts and the illusion of security.

It's easier to reset when we are young. During my freshman year of high school, I joined the cross-country team and found a place for myself as number seven on the team. The faster girls were all juniors and seniors, so as a freshman, it didn't occur to me to question my rank. We had a large team and being seventh was very respectable. About halfway through the season, we traveled to Upstate New York for a large invitational meet with dozens of other schools. I was very nervous as hundreds of girls lined up along the starting line and the gun went off with a crack. I set off at my usual pace. Out on the course, in a pretty meadow, I saw the bright yellow jersey of one of my teammates ahead of me. She was number six on the team and I was comforted to see that I was in my place as usual. But before we reached the end of the meadow, I was right on her heels and confronted with the fallibility of my belief that I was number seven. I found myself wondering, *Why couldn't I be number six?* So, I lengthened my stride and passed her easily. I went on to pass other yellow jerseys that day—number five and four and three and two. I ended that race in a new position as number two on the team. I never did beat number one that year, but I don't think it was because I had a limiting belief; she was just really, really fast.

Here is an absolute truth: We are born to [1] rule the roost of our reality, to shine bright.

this early in life. Some take half a lifetime to figure it out. Others (like me) go through several cycles of remembering how to live large and then forgetting again. And some never figure it out at all.

Where does the "live large" attitude come from? It's hard to imagine that little Abe put much thought into things on her first day with the others. Her attitude sprang fully formed from within her and she acted on it in ways that brought harmony to the group as a whole. Abe instinctively knew she was born to be part of a flock. She instinctively knew she had a right to defend and take up her space. She simply acted upon what she knew. The reason Abe was successful that day was precisely because she *didn't* think about it; she just *acted* from an indefinable yet very wise place within.

If we were to also live from that place, our actions would flow from our authentic selves—the part of us that touches infinity, the part that instinctively knows we are big and connected to something even bigger. We would see the world through the lens of peace, joy, and love while all of the judgments, fears, and insecurities of our ego mind would be left behind. We would stand tall, take up our space, and speak our truth. We would live boldly, using our minds as tools of creation instead of spinning fountains of worry. We would be free. A world filled with human beings who live this way would be the paradise we seek.

Little Abe planted a seed inside that maybe I too could stand tall and live my best life. Why was I living small? Despite the smiling face I showed to the world, why was I living with a secret, squirming ball of fear in my belly that only subsided when I had that first glass of wine each evening? What would it take to adopt a more powerful attitude, to become a proactive creator of my life rather than just reacting to the perceived expectations of myself and others?

While I certainly didn't change overnight, each day the chicks provided a positive focus that began to break through my limiting thoughts and emotion. Just by being their funny, fluffy little selves, they brought pure joy, giggles, and an expansive new light into my soul.

LESSON 5:

NOTICE THE DETAILS

I t was one of those long, lingering evenings that are the gift of summer. The air smelled like warm grass, spiced with salt the breeze carried from the harbor two blocks away. After a few more weeks in the big box on the dining room floor, our chickens were fully feathered and ready to go outside permanently.

The whole family had spent the day retrofitting the garden shed according to specifications I'd found online, with a little chicken-sized trap door for the birds to access their small fenced-in yard, a couple of nesting boxes, and a horizontal roosting pole six feet up because I had read that chickens like to sleep up high to be away from potential predators. As darkness came, we all got involved carrying the birds out one by one. Shanti escorted us as we made nine careful trips with a chicken tucked securely under an arm, or Mac-style with a squawking and flapping bird clutched between his outstretched hands. The more the chicken flapped and squawked, the bigger his gap-toothed grin grew.

As we put each bird up on the roosting pole, they stood there looking down at us, confused at first, softly murmuring little hums and clucks that seemed to be asking a question. But each stayed put as we added the others, completely trusting us to provide everything they needed. Once they settled themselves, lowering their soft bellies down over their feet, we said good night and shut the door. I took one last look through the window. The chickens blinked at me with sleepy eyes, seeming so at home already.

I felt proud that we were able to create such a nice space for them, a real chicken house. I was also deeply grateful that they accepted it so graciously. It was a delicious feeling to take care of something this way. It was different than taking care of children and I went to sleep wondering why that was.

The next morning, I couldn't wait to visit the chickens. I ran barefoot over the dewy grass with Shanti trotting happily beside me and looked in the window. The birds had been busy exploring their new space—some were sitting in a nesting box, others were on the floor drinking from their water bucket, and some were pecking at their food. I pulled on the rope that raised their trap door so they could go outside. They all went perfectly still for a moment before beginning to tip their heads from side to side, looking out. They clucked and commented excitedly to each other, stretching their necks out long to see the world better and, eventually, some took a few tentative steps forward.

I ran into the kitchen to grab a cup of coffee and then dragged an Adirondack chair over to the edge of the chicken fence where I could sit and watch. After a while, a brave black-and-white speckled chicken stuck its head out of the door and hopped down onto the ground. It cocked its head to look at me and took a few more steps. Another bird followed and soon they were all out in the sunshine, marveling at everything. It was all brand new to them.

A black one started scratching and found a worm. It leaned over to examine the wiggly thing before picking it up in its beak and giving it a shake. As if on cue, all the other birds ran over to see. The black chicken started running and the chase was on. There was tremendous squawking as Black was chased to the fence and forced to turn. One of the others grabbed the poor worm from Black's beak and started running the other way. The rest followed, of course, and the fracas continued until one of the chickens eventually swallowed the worm with a gulp. Then everything stopped. They stared for a moment, blinking. Then, one by one, they each shook their feathers and proceeded to mill about some more, sampling the vegetation. It quickly became clear that clover was their favorite. After one taste of clover, a bird would eat every leaf off the plant in a wild flurry.

They explored their new world with great gusto, trying different bugs and jumping up to taste leaves that grew over their heads. I couldn't get enough of watching them be delighted.

That evening, and every evening afterward, the chickens put themselves to bed up on the roosting pole. It was quite a sight to look up and see them perched there, all lined up with their fluffy underbellies exposed. They tilted their heads whenever we came in to check on them and made soft cooing *baaalk, baaalk, bak* noises. It would occur to me in those dusky moments that the chickens were perfectly content.

One afternoon, as I was sitting at my desk avoiding my work and gobbling cashews by the fistful, my overheated brain started noodling on this vision of contented chickens. The more I procrastinated, the more the ball of worry in my belly throbbed, but nonetheless, my brain wanted to think about chickens.

Many people think of chickens as not particularly bright, but I wondered: *Who was the stupid one?* I was a worrying, scurrying, multitasking fool with my college education and big brain, and the chickens—with a brain the size of a soybean—seemed to possess the joyful peace of the Buddha. I wanted some of that.

Why was contentment so elusive for me? Shouldn't I have at least as much joy as a chicken? What was their secret?

This inquiry sprang up in my mind with a refreshing splash, as if I'd stumbled upon a clear mountain spring. My cashew gobbling stopped as an answer bubbled up. What came was an observation that the tiny brain of a chicken seemed to only focus on one detail at a time—Look! A beetle! Ping! Beetle is in beak! Snap! Beetle is in gizzard! Yum!

My big brain, on the other hand, hardly ever noticed the details—it was too flooded with thoughts, most of which were negative. It constantly spun anxiety-producing stories about things that could go wrong in the future. It churned with resentments and swamped me with regurgitations of various hurts and shameful events from my past. The terrifying thing was that I didn't feel like these thoughts were a choice; they seemed to arise out of nowhere, unbidden, and run around in my head making a shitty mess of me—even while I slept.

How could I ever be happy against such an onslaught? How could I stop it? Maybe there was a better way to use my big brain—a way that favored conscious reflection upon thoughts I *chose* rather than relentless subconscious rumination about thoughts that chose me.

Taking a page from the chickens' playbook, I decided to start noticing the details right then and there. I looked into my can of cashews and carefully chose one, just *one*, that was whole and nearly perfect. I took the nut out of the can and studied it, admiring its shape and texture, and decided to do nothing, to not even *think* about anything except enjoying the cashew for as long as it took me to chew and swallow it. I was on the third one before I realized I hadn't succeeded yet. While I chewed, my hands flitted around, picking up paper clips, straightening piles, cleaning a fingernail. My mind kept drifting to my to-do list, to a resentful thought about Paul, to my dread over an approaching deadline. How could it be that accomplishing a single focus for all of 40 seconds was so difficult? Finally, I sat on my hands, forced my eyes closed and enjoyed the complete experience of chewing and swallowing a single cashew without allowing myself to be distracted. I felt victorious.

My victory was short-lived, of course. Some part of me was apparently totally addicted to multitasking, to thinking about negative things, and I was right back at it within two minutes. But at least now I had a tool for taking a break from my normal frenzied self—if only I could remember to use it.

The next time Shanti wandered by, I noticed. I stopped working and called her to me. She came over and sat, looking up at me expectantly, seeming puzzled by the sudden attention. She put a paw on my knee and cocked her head. I looked into her sparkly dark brown eyes and focused on the sensations of my fingertips as I stroked the soft curls on her floppy ears.

How perfectly lovely it was to be in such a moment!

A deep breath flowed in as I held her paw and a wave of relaxation washed away some of the tension that I held in my body, tension I hadn't even known was there. I desperately wanted more of this feeling, and yet in the next instant my thoughts ran away with me again, and Shanti returned to her bed for a nap.

Why was it so hard for me to focus on the things that made me happy? *I must be insane,* I thought.

My frustration with this caused me to start asking other people about their experience and I learned I was not alone. Apparently, people have been struggling with this problem since the dawn of time. We are all insane together.

"Meditate," I heard someone say on TV. "Clear your mind of all thoughts." Yeah, right— the immense pressure of the jumble of thoughts that attacked when I tried to do that nearly killed me. I couldn't imagine anything sucking more. Trying to meditate made me feel even crazier.

"Pray," said an acquaintance (who honestly didn't seem any saner than I was). Hmm. Lovely idea, but my version of praying then was to hold my hand in the air with the palm facing upward and say, "No thanks, God. Go help someone who needs it." My arrogant conviction that I had things all figured out had always been so firm, that I didn't think God would be open to a conversation.

"Yoga, that's what you need," said a serene friend who dragged me to a class one day. This certainly was a strange new world—one that involved being very quiet and moving at sloth-like speeds. For me, it was tortuously hard to downshift so dramatically—like driving a speeding car and then slamming it into first gear. It was too much for my nervous system to take on that day, but I could see the promise it held.

My brother turned out to be the first to offer a doable-for-me answer to my cry for help by sending an audio recording of Wayne Dyer's book *The Power of Intention*. I was spellbound; the ideas made so much sense as I listened to them that I was sure I was cured. It explained everything!! Whenever I stopped listening, however, my frantic whacko thoughts returned. I'd listen to the book on the drive to work and feel so happy and free when I parked my car, but by the time I had finished climbing the stairs to my third-floor office, the monkeys in my mind would once again be swinging from the trees. I went back out to my car each day at lunchtime so I could get another hit of sanity. I bought a CD player I could hook to my belt loop so I could listen when I walked and did house chores. I listened myself to sleep. I just kept listening. And when I was done with the book, I listened to it again.

Over time, I found I could hold my focus on the details I chose longer and longer. This always quieted my mind. Soaking in the details grounded me firmly in the present moment—I'd never understood what that meant before—and in those moments, just like the chickens, I was content.

Whenever I could, I took Shanti on long walks through a beautiful cemetery on top of the hill overlooking the harbor. I practiced being content there. Tucked away from noisy streets and houses, the cemetery offered a secluded place for wandering quietly amongst giant trees and rhododendron bushes. I marveled at the flowers and the leaves, the birds, even the bugs. My skin registered the sensations of the breezes, the sunlight, the rain. Majestic marble and granite stones lined the meandering paths, each standing guard over a life that had been reduced to simple carvings of names and dates. I found myself studying those carvings, tracing them with my fingers, and allowing my imagination to spin a story about the lived life. Observing the details in such a place inspired a newfound practice of awe, which made it easier to release my fusty old habits of thought.

This growing ability to choose where I placed my attention opened up many avenues for improving my existence. It made sense that the more of my mind I reclaimed, the more resources I would have available to continue to improve. The chickens had shown me a way to begin an upward spiral out of the madness and into the light—moment by moment.

With this new level of awareness, I watched the children as they moved around the kitchen in an ordinary moment one afternoon. I allowed myself to notice the details of their actions. I saw Tom's confidence as he stirred something in a pot; Patrick's funniness as he said something silly yet profound; Katie's sweetness as she helped her brother pour some milk; and Mac's bright smile as he told a secret to the dog. I relaxed into appreciating all that was good about them and focused on just *being with* them rather than my usual obsessive *worrying about* them. They seemed to like it.

I came to see that my worrying did nothing to help get things done and it probably even hurt. Worry fueled my anxiety and destroyed my ability to see solutions. Worry made me tense and crabby. Worry compelled me to jump in and fix things that would have been best left to others to fix. Worry wore me out. The chickens certainly didn't worry.

There was one idea from Wayne Dyer, in particular, that has stuck with me over the years: *Do what you ought and trust what may be.* I used it to cure my habit of worry. Whenever I found myself worrying, I thought about what actions I could take to help with whatever issue I was worried about. Once I had done what I could—which was often nothing—I just trusted whatever happened next. If some problem required my attention in the future, I would deal with it then, rather than pollute my brain with impotent worry about it now.

As I released more and more of my obsessive worrying, I was able to notice other types of thoughts that made my body tense up: judgments and expectations. These popped into my head at the speed of light, it seemed, one after the other. Nothing was ever good enough for me. I know I didn't start out that way and I don't remember ever choosing to be that way, but I couldn't deny the truth of it—this habit of thought was firmly entrenched.

One day while walking in the cemetery with Shanti, I found myself flipping through a long mental list of things that the kids should or should not be doing. I didn't intend to be doing this during my beautiful walk time, but it's where my mind took me. *Tom should work harder at painting the trim on the house. Patrick should not play on the computer so much. Mac should stop losing his homework papers. Katie shouldn't—*

I caught myself and froze.

Ahhh, I thought, *so that's the difference between caring for the kids and caring for the chickens. I don't feel any need to* judge *the chickens.* The chickens never disappointed me because I never created an expectation about them. They were free to just be chickens and I was free to simply enjoy them.

Who would I be without expectations? What would happen if I wasn't always trying to teach and push the children to be "better" so they could fulfill my hopes for them? What part of how they do things is my responsibility anyway?

From inside the habit, it was hard to see how our lives could be okay if I ceased to expect anything, but fueled by my success in reducing my worrying ways, I decided it was worth a try. It was terrifying at first, like driving down a slippery, dark road and taking my hands off the steering wheel, but my new intention made me aware of the physical sensations that came over me whenever I allowed an expectation to form. Under the influence of an expectation, the muscles between my shoulder blades wound themselves up tight as if I was actually *steering* people and situations toward my will. This had created such chronic tension over the years that my upper spine had been painfully pulled out of alignment. I'd found relief with the chiropractor, but his adjustments only lasted a day before my controlling mind would cause my muscles to throw things off again.

Once I became aware of this sensation, I learned to look for and name the judgmental thought that was causing it. When the negative thought was about one of the children, I found I could replace it with a vision of the child living his or her best life, whatever that meant *to them*.

I came to understand that a child's life is not mine to control. They have lessons to learn, consequences to bear, and soul paths to explore that have nothing to do with my definition of success. Guidance and correction are sometimes necessary, of course, but those are best administered in a given *moment*. I certainly didn't need to carry the expectations and judgments around in my body *all the friggin' time*. I learned to think like a sheepdog, who may occasionally need to nip at a few heels to steer lambs away from the edge of a cliff, but who then heads off without a care to take a nap in the shade.

In these ways, learning from the chickens was literally rewiring my brain to favor noticing and appreciating the juicy and present details of my life over my old critical ways. As some of the chronic tension left my body, I enjoyed better sleep and more moments of true relaxation.

During that summer and fall, I never tired of watching the chickens put themselves to bed. I found it enchanting how they knew when they should stop exploring their little yard and return to the security of their little shed. The chickens' single-mindedness allowed them to take very good care of themselves—and they were teaching me to do the same.

LESSON 6:

EMBRACE THE NATURAL WAY OF THINGS

As the chickens matured, it began to dawn on me that maybe I had gotten more than my fair share of roosters. For the first few months as they morphed from little balls of fluff into birds with actual feathers, they appeared genderless. Aside from their color—three of the birds were black, a shiny ebony with a touch of rainbow iridescence; one was white; and the rest were gray with white flecks— they all looked pretty much the same. They even all grew that wobbly red stuff on their heads. But then I began to notice that some were growing longer tail feathers. Were these the roosters? Or was this just due to the ragtag bunch of breeds in my little flock? For a few more weeks, they had me guessing.

Then the crowing started.

At first, there were only a few extra squawks that were a bit more aggressive than their usual noises, but as the days went on, I listened more closely and realized that they were adding syllables. What had started as a long *raaaaaaaw* turned into *raaaw caa*, and then *raaw caa errrr errrr*, and finally what we all think of as *cock-a-doodle-doo*.

Soon there were not just one or two rowdy roosters crowing cock-a-doodle-doo, but six. Six! *Six* of my nine birds were roosters. This realization landed with a thud. Not only wasn't this fair given the laws of probability that only half of the chickens would be male, I had another problem: I had neighbors all around. There were seven houses within 200 feet of my chicken coop. There would surely be complaints about all the noise; town ordinances would probably be invoked and that would be the end of my beloved chickens.

I went to each of my neighbors and apologized, explaining that I would take care of the problem and thanking them in advance for their patience. Some were actually delighted. These families had immigrated to America from the Azores, the beautiful islands off the coast of Portugal, and they told me the noises reminded them of the Old Country. The chickens brought us closer to those who had always kept their distance from us—before the chickens, we were known as "The English" and watched with suspicion. The Portuguese couple who lived next door had held us at arm's length for years—barely nodding when we said hello—but they lit up when I explained about the chickens. They asked in broken

English if they could visit them. After that, I often found them standing in our backyard, holding hands and gazing at the birds. All this peace and love caused me to breathe a sigh of relief for the short term, but I knew I still had a problem: I couldn't keep six roosters on our small bit of property.

So on the next visit to the farm, I told David that I would be bringing over some roosters for him.

"But I don't want your roosters," he said simply.

My jaw flapped open. "What do you mean you don't want my roosters?" I said, shocked. "They're beautiful!"

"Nobody is going to want your roosters," he said with a small, compassionate smile.

I blinked, taking a moment to digest that information. "Well, then, what do I do with them?"

"You could kill them and eat them," he suggested helpfully.

I felt my knees wobble and my breath catch. "Oh my God," I said.

I stumbled to my car and got out of there fast.

The next week, when Mac and I returned to the farm, my problem was a bit louder as my roosters had attained greater crowing proficiency.

After the chores were done, I found David and strode up to him confidently. "Okay," I said, taking a deep breath. "I get it that roosters aren't in big demand. And I think it might be okay to eat them, but I can't kill them. Would you kill them for me?"

"Yes," he said after a pause. "I'll kill them for you."

"Thank you," I mumbled, fighting a wave of nausea.

I drove home and curled myself into a tight and troubled ball on the couch. Nothing about that solution felt right.

Over the next week, I uncurled a bit and by the time I saw David again I was feeling very brave. "David," I said quickly in hopes that I could get this out before I lost my nerve. "I really think that the most honest thing is for me to go ahead and kill them myself. It's too much of a cop-out to ask you to do it for me."

"Okay," he said calmly, missing entirely the chance to *insist* that he do it for me.

I gulped privately before soldiering on. "Umm, how would I go about doing it? How do *you* do it?"

"Well," he spoke in his quiet teacher's tone, "I just chop off their heads."

WAAA! HOLY SHIT!!! my whole being screamed silently, every nerve on high alert. "Right," I said, trying to match his calmness. "Doesn't the blood gush everywhere?"

"Yes, a bit, but then it stops."

"So after you kill it, then what?" I asked as *my* blood left *my* head. "I mean, how do you make it ready to eat?"

"First, I take the feathers off and then I take the insides out and it's done. It's not difficult."

"Okay," I said in a very small voice.

There was no longer anywhere to hide.

Over the next couple of days, I tried to visualize the act of killing a rooster—one of *my precious* roosters. I seriously couldn't see myself chopping the head off of anything with an axe simply because I knew I wasn't that good with an axe. Plus, it didn't sound very nice for the chicken. *No,* I thought, *there must be more than one way to kill a chicken.* So, I went to Google and typed "how to kill a chicken." There were a large number of hits—8,604,712 to be exact—many with step-by-step instructions and pictures. It turned out that there are indeed many ways to kill a chicken. All I had to do was pick one.

I obsessed over this decision, becoming increasingly fixated and delirious. I read and reread the instructions to try to get comfortable with the steps involved. I finally decided upon a method that involved tying the bird upside down by his feet and slitting his throat. Believe it or not, this sounded like the most peaceful method as the blood would leave the brain very quickly and it would all be over.

I visualized myself doing it over and over again. My dreams were haunted. I talked to everyone who would listen and told them what I was going to do. Talking about it made me less likely to, um, chicken out. It also put things in perspective. As I told my Portuguese neighbors, I discovered that most were very familiar with the process. "Oh, yes," said four-and-a-half-foot-tall Anna with a grin and a twinkle in her eye. "I used to help my grandmother kill the chickens when I was a little girl in the Azores." *Silly English,* they all seemed to be thinking. *Killing a chicken is the most natural thing in the world. What's the big deal?*

The fact is that killing something and then eating it has actually become a Very Big Deal for most of us. As "civilized" people, we have lost the wildness that would make this act as natural as breathing. We breathe in; we breathe out. We kill; we eat. This is somewhere in our DNA. Our ancestors obviously did it or we would not be here. In just a couple of generations, though, we have forgotten where our food comes from, allowing ourselves to believe that it comes from pretty plastic-wrapped packages at the grocery store. We breathe in; we breathe out. We *shop*; we eat. It's all very tidy and nice, but it is not the natural way of things.

As the realness of what I was about to do loomed, I decided it was time for action. I spent a day gathering what I'd need and setting up the backyard. I worked by myself; it never occurred to me to ask for help—I didn't *want* help. This sacred task needed to be done alone.

There was comfort in the motion of the physical work required to get everything ready. First, I dug a hole at the back of the fence to catch the blood. Then I found a straight, sturdy stick and tied it up horizontally across the top corner of the fence over the hole for hanging the chicken by his feet. This would be the ideal height if I knelt while doing the deed, which had the added benefit of making me closer to the ground if I fainted. I found a length of rope, gathered a pile of wood to burn, and selected a couple of knives of different sizes. For the scalding step that loosens the feathers for plucking, I bought a large pot I could use to heat water over a fire. I put new batteries in a flashlight and lined a large trash can with a garbage bag. Finally, I printed out my step-by-step instructions. I had thought of everything.

It was time.

I went to bed early on that Friday night and slept fitfully, looking at the clock every few hours to make sure I didn't miss the chance to complete my mission before sunrise. I had read that chickens are calmer before dawn and it made some sense to me that it might be better to kill a calm chicken than an uptight one. I felt both desperately anxious and oddly curious. I longed to get the whole thing over with, and yet, I was immensely interested in the process and how I would handle it. At four o'clock in the morning, I gave up sleeping, dressed quickly, and went out to the backyard.

It was pitch-black, well before dawn during that early part of September, and quite warm, with a wet wind whipping heavy clouds over my head. It smelled like rain. I went first to the fire pit, struck a match, and held it to the tender corners of the newspaper and tinder I had arranged the day before. I watched as the flame flashed hot to consume the paper and begin to snap at the wood. Once I was convinced the fire had caught, I went over to the horizontal pole to make sure it was secure and that the rope was all set. I rehearsed how I would secure the chicken by his feet in the gentlest way.

Then I added wood to the fire and set the pot of water on the grate to boil. I took a deep breath. I felt an odd quiet inside, mixed with a clammy fear. *How was it possible to feel both at once?* My feet seemed to carry me around like they had more understanding of what was required than my brain did. I walked to the chicken house and opened the door. I shone the flashlight up to the rafters. There they were. I did not feel or think as I gently took what I knew to be the noisiest rooster off the roosting pole, placed him under my arm, and carried him outside. I closed the door behind me. The other birds cooed softly. The bird in my hands clucked and started to flap his wings. I turned him upside down and held him by his feet. He quieted when held like that, just like I had read.

I carried him over to the horizontal pole. I grabbed the cord and tried to wrap it around his feet. He flapped vigorously at one point and tried to peck my hand, but I kept on wrapping his feet. I spoke to him quietly, saying things like "I am sorry, darling bird" and "I will be gentle with you" repeatedly. Finally, he was hanging there in the darkness. I got on my knees, which made my head level with his. I looked at him. He blinked at me with an upside-down eye. *Oh my...*I decided a prayer was in order. Still quite sure God wasn't listening to me, I kept it short: "Thank you, God— or whatever—for sharing this beautiful rooster with me. I honor him and you." My breathing felt peculiar; it was as if I wasn't actually breathing, but rather I was *being breathed*. The chicken flounced once and his foot came out of its wrappings. My breath caught in my throat and I quickly retied him. I lifted the knife and took his head in my hand. I tilted his head away from me to expose the area right under the ear that I needed to slice. I pressed the knife to the spot and cut. It didn't slice. I tried to cut again, but only the slightest cut was made. *Oh my God*, my whole being wailed silently. *Oh my God, Ohmygod, ohmygod, ohmygod,* I murmured over and over again, absolutely panicked. While it had worked fine for tomatoes, the knife wasn't sharp enough to cut through the loose rubbery flesh of the rooster's neck! I couldn't stop now to get another knife, so I started sawing away, knowing that if I couldn't cut clean, I had to cut fast so it would go as quickly as possible for him. *Ohmigod, ohmigod, ohmigod. I'm so sorry. I'm so sorry. I'm so sorry. Sorrysorrysorry.* Tears streamed down my face. It began to rain. I felt his eye blink against my palm. When I knew I had cut enough, I held his head still while the rain poured down and the blood drained out into the earth below. I was shaking with grief and horror at what I had done. I took a deep breath. *Okayokayokay*, I said to myself repeatedly, trying to keep my grip on sanity.

And then a remarkable thing happened. I was suddenly flooded with a comforting peace, like the warmth of the sun after a chill. Words can't accurately describe the sensation, but I swear the rooster found a way to communicate with me. He seemed to say, *"Aw, come on now. Don't worry about it, honey. This is what chickens do. We've been doing this for thousands and thousands of years."*

It took me a couple of days to understand what had happened in that moment. My rooster had died with grace. As prey animals, chickens have a role in the food chain and they accept death as a natural part of their life, as natural as breathing or eating or pooping. At an elemental level, my rooster understood his purpose, and after offering the barest resistance, he simply accepted it. As predators, we have no such deal with death. We conclude that dying is not part of our purpose, so we fight it in every way we can. And yet, it always finds us anyway.

Where does death fit into our purpose? I wondered. No answers came to me that morning as I took a life into my own hands and ended it on purpose, for a purpose.

I simply became empty—a vessel waiting to be filled.

LESSON 7:

WHERE FOOD COMES FROM

As I stood in the dark on that wet Saturday morning, I felt numb, but driven to complete the task of making my rooster ready to eat that night. It was very important to me that his death not be wasted. So, I pressed on through the steps I had printed out and practiced in my mind.

The rain was coming down hard as I untied him and carried him over to the large pot of steaming water. I took the lid off and held him gingerly by his feet as I dunked the rest of him. I swirled him around a bit and then pulled him out. The air smelled of boiled chicken—my first clue that perhaps my water was too hot. The rain flowed down my face as I stood in the dark holding a hot, wet dead bird in my hands.

I sat down in a soaked Adirondack chair and started plucking feathers. The world record for plucking a chicken is 4.4 seconds, but I wasn't so practiced and whoever set that record probably wasn't plucking in a downpour. While the feathers came off my bird easily, they stuck to my wet fingers as I tried to put them in the trash can. I pulled feathers off the bird and then off my hand and then off my other hand and then off my first hand again and so on. It was slow going. When I finally reached the wing, I kept a few of the longest, most beautiful feathers to remind me of this rooster and this day.

After about 20 minutes of plucking, I had a naked bird with much of its parboiled skin ready to come off too. I squinted in the predawn gloom to see my instructions, now soggy from the rain. The next step was to cut off the feet. I placed the carcass on a pad of newspaper on the picnic table, took my (hopefully sharper) butcher's knife, and cut his perfect bright yellow feet off at the joint where drumsticks begin. I threw the feet into the trash can and looked down at them lying there in the bottom for a long moment as my overstimulated brain grappled with how weird it is to see feet in the trash.

The next step said, *Remove the head*, so I did. I held it over the trash and froze—my hands were unable to perform the act of dropping the head into the bucket. This must be why hunters mount the heads of the animals they kill—eyes shouldn't be in the trash. I took a breath and dropped it in. I stared in after it. There was the head with its eyes, right next to the bright yellow feet. I felt sick. *Keep going, keep going, keepgoing, keepgoing.*

I swallowed panic and turned back to my instructions. Next, I was supposed to cut the neck at the shoulders "while being careful of the crop." I hesitated here. *What was a crop?* My instructions weren't clear. I was supposed to know what a crop was and I didn't. I thought it would be obvious. I felt around at the base of the now headless neck and couldn't feel anything that might be a crop. I looked at the instructions again. After several seconds of wondering what to do, I shrugged and made a cut next to the shoulders.

Next step: *Remove the oil gland from the back of the tail. Be careful not to cut it or it will make the meat bitter.* Oops. What oil gland? Again, I thought it would be obvious. I studied the picture closely, blinking the rain out of my eyes, and cut where it told me to cut, hoping for the best. I cut a slit from the "keel or breastbone to the anus, around the anus, and back to the original cut" (this is much harder to figure out than it sounds).

Next, it was time to pull the guts out. I rolled up my sleeve and stuck my hand inside, loosened what I hoped was the esophagus as the directions instructed, then gathered up all sorts of warm, slippery bits, and pulled. The whole mess came out as a set and lay there glistening on the wet newspaper. As I stared at it in the half-light of dawn, I decided it wasn't a mess at all; it was a fascinating conglomeration of parts and plumbing—the heart and the liver, the kidneys and the testes, the gall bladder and the lungs, the gizzard and intestines—they were all there. It was impressive to see how everything fit inside the space within a chicken. How could such a spectacular feat of engineering and efficiency be a random accident of evolution?

I poked the liver with my finger. I remembered my mother cooking chicken livers for us when I was a kid. They were delicious, all fried and crispy with soft, creamy, rich insides. It had never occurred to me to buy chicken livers myself. Did they even sell them anymore? They were probably filled with toxins these days anyway. But I knew this rooster's liver wasn't, so I separated it from the rest and put it aside.

Now I looked at my bird. It looked amazingly like a whole chicken I would buy at the grocery store, except much scrawnier. And, of course, the skin was all puffy from being boiled, but still, a really good first effort. I took it inside, rinsed it off, and put it in a tub of ice in the refrigerator.

As the refrigerator door closed, I stood still in the kitchen and felt myself vibrate with an odd inner hum. Now that it was done, the emotions I had held in check so I could get through the process drifted toward me like a creeping fog. I looked at the clock. It was six-thirty and the rain was still coming down hard. The dreary day was as bright as it was going to get. What was I to do with myself now? I had to keep moving. The whole family was still asleep. I decided to go to the gym; maybe I could work off my shakiness.

The light seemed strange as I drove to the gym, and I had a floaty, underwater feeling. I stretched, ran on the treadmill, pressed heavy weights, and tried to be interested in what was on the overhead televisions, but nothing helped. I was disconnected from the world. Finally, I took a shower and drove home, still vibrating with a heavy buzz that wouldn't let me take a full breath.

I was in new territory, stretched beyond myself, almost out of my body. What was happening to me? Was I possessed by the chicken? Thoughts and images flowed like a dream out of control:

Beautiful-bird-with-the-blinking-eye.
My bird. Patient. Trusting.
Be-so-GentleGentleGentle.
Except-not-gentle-at-all!
OhMyGod. Ohmygod. Ohmygod.
Horror.
Loving. Loving. Loving-some-more.
Keep-on-moving-and-everything-will-be-okay.
Beokay-beokay. Be. Okay.

Once home, I made myself a cup of coffee, but that didn't help. I felt adrift. Doing normal things, talking to normal people about their normal lives seemed so silly to me now. My own life seemed silly. I had let go of reality as I knew it and gone back to something more primal, from an earlier time, when work meant using your body and food walked and squawked and died with grace right before your eyes. Back when people ate off the land and it was enough. There was something so right and clean and bright about it and yet so *foreign* to the life I had created in my downtown existence.

I thrummed and throbbed around the house for the rest of the morning, interacting with my family through a thick fog of wonder and despair.

In the early afternoon, desperate for a normal activity, I walked to the consignment shop a few blocks away. My friend Roxanne owned the shop and was one of the many people I had told about what I was going to do that morning. The little bells chimed as I opened the door and she looked up from her perch behind the register.

Her large brown eyes grew larger when she saw me. "You look very affected," she said with concern.

"I am," I said quietly. "I am." I fought back a gush of tears.

Roxanne asked what had happened and I told her. I barely noticed the bells sounding as another woman opened and closed the door, but as I finished telling my story, the woman approached us. She was petite with short gray hair worn in an elegant cut; a light burned brightly in her sky-blue eyes.

"You know," she said, "I overheard the conflict you feel about what happened today and I'd like to offer a different perspective if that's okay with you."

"Sure," I said numbly.

She continued, "I work for a world hunger organization and we've learned over the years that while we can survive, humans can't thrive without animal protein and fats. It's a necessary part of our optimal diet." She put the slacks she was carrying down on a stool and took a step closer to me, comforting me with her presence. "One way to look at it is that we're all here to serve one another," she said matter-of-factly. "We take care of the animals and they nourish us."

I could feel a seed take hold inside of me, a barely perceptible lightening of my heart, like what I had miraculously felt each time I had conceived a child. For a brief eternal moment, I was overcome by a knowing hush that pushed out awareness of all else. She had articulated something that I felt when I had previously attempted to live as a vegetarian, an experiment that spanned years and resulted in anemia and overall weakness. Simply put, I had failed to thrive without meat.

I thanked this woman with a gratitude that came from my toes. I knew that what she had just shared with me was very important and very true. It felt like destiny that she had appeared in that store on that day with that perfect message for me. As her words settled into my core, I realized that there was no chicken on the planet that I had more of a right to kill and eat than the chicken I had nurtured since he was a yolk.

That evening I sautéed the rooster in olive oil, garlic, and white wine. I served him with basmati rice and broccoli. We sat at the table and I made a point of saying a blessing for the bird before beginning to eat it. I put a piece in my mouth and chewed. The meat tasted like chicken, except *more*. Much more. The chickens found at the grocery store tasted like water in comparison. This chicken, *our* chicken, was delicious! But it was also tough. I chewed and chewed, absorbing the flavor, and eventually swallowed when I got tired of chewing. It was like swallowing leather. (I learned later that I had left out the important step of letting the meat age for a day or two to allow the muscle fibers to relax after rigor mortis.) I looked around the table to see my family chewing and swallowing hard without a word of complaint. They knew how important this was to me and I loved them for it. Their brave solemn smiles made my eyes well with tears of gratitude.

As my body absorbed the nutrients offered by the rooster, my mind absorbed the concepts and philosophies the experience had forced me to confront. We had provided the chicken with life itself and given him five months of sunshine and organic chicken pellets and fresh, clear water and grass and clover and bugs and companionship. We had raised the chicken in love, and I had ended his life in love and, for the first time in a very long time, I ate consciously, appreciating and loving every morsel of the food I was consuming.

I had never felt so alive.

LESSON 8:

PROVIDENCE MOVES TOO

As September wore on, my remaining raucous roosters continued to rattle the neighborhood. Clearly, I still had a problem.

I quickly decided that killing one bird was all I could handle for the near term and rededicated myself to finding a new home for my roosters. I didn't really know where to begin. I wanted to be sure that they didn't end up in the hands of some cruel cockfight aficionados. If they couldn't run around a barnyard somewhere doing what roosters do, then I wanted them to be killed humanely and eaten with appreciation and gusto.

With that commitment in mind, I spread the word to anyone who would listen. With my newfound calm, I didn't worry about it; I knew down deep that the solution would appear. After all, I'd been provided with everything I needed at every step of the way ever since I had committed myself to those eggs and put them in the incubator.

Commitment is a powerful force. I first became conscious of this many years earlier while visiting my mother at the college where she taught in Burlington, Vermont. At the time I was pregnant with Tom, my first child, which I had noticed had the lovely effect of inspiring people to want to take care of me (and of inspiring me to let them). So while she finished up her last class, a professor friend of hers invited me into his office for a chat. Mike was an expansive and generous guy with lots of interesting ideas to share. Before too long, I found myself curled up in a chair, watching in fascination as he showed me how to use a pendulum to predict the sex of my baby. I cannot remember whether the pendulum's prediction about my boy child was correct, but he ended up giving me an even more important awareness. When Mom stuck her head in the door later to tell me she was ready to go, Mike frantically searched his office for a parting gift for me and ended up pushing a copy of a short-lived magazine called *Creating Excellence* into my hands.

Later that night when I looked at the magazine before sleeping, I found a quote about commitment on the inside front cover. The quote was excerpted from W.H. Murray's 1951 book, *The Scottish Himalayan Expedition*. Murray, a contemporary of Edmund Hillary, was part of the team that discovered a route that would eventually lead to Hillary's first successful climb of Mount Everest in 1953. Murray had also been a German prisoner of war in Africa during World War II, where he ended up writing two drafts of his

book *Mountaineering in Scotland*—the second on
after the first was confiscated by his captors. Thi
ing man knew a thing or two about commitment. He
what he wrote:

> Until one is committed, there is hesitancy, the chance
> to draw back, always ineffectiveness.
>
> Concerning all acts of initiative (and creation), there
> is one elementary truth, the ignorance of which kills
> countless ideas and splendid plans:
>
> The moment one definitely commits oneself, then
> Providence moves too. All sorts of things occur to
> help one that would never otherwise have occurred.
> A whole stream of events issues from the decision,
> raising in one's favor all manner of unforeseen
> incidents and meetings and material assistance, which
> no man could have dreamt would have come his way.
>
> I learned a deep respect for one of Goethe's couplets:
>
> Whatever you can do or dream you can, begin it.
> Boldness has genius, power and magic in it!

My 27-year-old self felt the truth in that quote deeply
enough to rip it out of the magazine and post it on the wall
next to my desk. Over the years, I've reread it hundreds of

/ith anyone who seemed to need its
↳ò all in. *You will be met and given all you*

..is principle again and again during those
..e when I was faced with an opportunity that
..t has always proven true. There were also long
years—like those years before the chickens came to me—
when I've forgotten about it and languished in a purposeless,
commitment-less, and Providence-free void.

The trick, I've found, is to have something worth committing to—whether that's an interest, a passion, a person, a
practice, a journey, a pet, a patch of land, a pot of basil, a part
in a play, or a bunch of fertilized eggs. The miracles that come
from committing only happen *after* I leap into the unknown.

We all must learn to leap. If you feel drawn to getting a
dog, for example, then leap into the process of finding your
perfect canine companion. Just do it. Do it now and don't
look back. Don't be dissuaded by all of the sensible reasons
not to get a dog for there are always so many.

It's *always* easier to stay where things are safe and comfortable; where you don't have anything else to worry about;
where you'll never have to clean poop off your carpet; where
you can leave a stack of magazines next to the couch and
know that they won't be chewed to bits when you return.
But while it is true that everything may stay nice and neat,
you are also robbed of all of the heart emotions that make
life so rich. Maybe you'll be spared the brief upset of seeing a
wet spot on the floor, but you'll miss the joyful, over-the-top

greeting when you walk through the door, the giggle you just can't suppress when your toes are being nibbled, and the quiet companionship when no one else cares. You will miss being unconditionally loved by your own very special being.

For all of the sensible reasons our minds come up with for us to sit still and stay safe, the glimmers keep returning, don't they? Little sparkly thoughts that intrigue us with their "maybe someday" promise. *Maybe someday I'll take up painting. Maybe someday I'll get a cat. Maybe someday I'll stand on a mountaintop in China. Maybe someday I'll quit my awful job. Maybe someday I'll grow a lemon tree in my dining room. Maybe someday I'll live on a small farm. Maybe someday...*But *maybe someday* never comes to us; we have to start walking toward it.

We are blessed with time on this earth so that we can stretch, grow, and Live with a capital "L." The only way we can lose is to stay so safe and clean that we blow our opportunity. A life well lived means committing to things that may be messy—they may piss us off, hurt our feelings, or make us cry—but we also get to experience more of the heart-swelling joy that comes when we grab onto such opportunities with both hands, hold on tight, and allow Providence to do her thing.

Soon after I put the word out about the roosters, Tom came home from high school one day with a possible solution to my problem. "My friend Manny's uncle has chickens and might want your roosters."

So I called Manny's uncle and he agreed to take them. "Some might go into the pot," he warned, "but I might keep one or two if I like how they get along with the rest of my flock." I wasn't going to get a better deal than that.

Even though I was happy to have found a solution, the sadness I felt about saying goodbye to my five remaining roosters weighed heavily. I went out to the coop and carefully placed the birds into sturdy boxes. The three hens looked a bit confused as I turned to go. I blinked back tears. "It's okay, girls. We've still got each other," I said as I closed the door behind me.

I kept up a comforting monologue throughout the half-hour ride to Manny's uncle's farm in Westport, Massachusetts. I was soothing myself more than the roosters, of course, but they occasionally clucked or cooed in polite response. I found the mailbox Manny's uncle had described and pulled into his driveway. "Okay, boys, here we are! Your new home. You can make as much noise as you want here!" I said with extra bravado as I swallowed hard against the ravaging forces of grief threatening to assail my heart.

I stopped in front of the house and started unloading the boxes as Manny's uncle came out to greet me. We took the boxes back to his chicken pen along the edge of the woods, where there was lots of room for my roosters to run around and lots of hens to chase. He opened the door that let us inside the wire fence and we released the birds. They stood there blinking for a few seconds before starting to explore. I folded my arms and hugged myself tight so I wouldn't explode into tears in front of Manny's uncle.

His two roosters didn't like the new competition and quickly ran over to show my birds who ruled *this* roost. My white rooster, definitely the most handsome and cocky of the bunch, fluffed himself up big and asserted himself mightily. One of the speckled gray-and-whites did the same. The others tried to pretend they were hens. This made us both laugh. I hugged myself harder.

We watched for a while as they sorted things out. "I might keep the white one and that one there," said Manny's uncle, pointing at another handsome bird. "The others will probably become stew relatively soon."

I appreciated his honesty and was glad they would be treated well during their remaining days, however many or few. I thanked him in a wobbly voice and started gathering my boxes to leave when he said, "Wait."

He deftly grabbed one of his hens, despite her squawking protest, and put her in a box. Then he grabbed another, and another, and stuck them both in with the first. He folded the flaps of the box securely and handed it to me. "Take these with you," he said.

I was amazed and grateful. "Thank you so much!"

I drove home that day with three more hens to add to my bunch and a heart so full of love and delighted surprise that I couldn't stop smiling.

Providence had once again moved for me.

LESSON 9:

LOVE IS A NUTRIENT

A young hen won't lay her first egg until she is about six months old, so my little girls still didn't know about such grown-up things. But after welcoming the three older ladies, they had joined right in with celebrating whenever one of them laid an egg. This was a loud hen party of achievement that occurred *every single time—Bak bakbak-bak BAK BAK BAKKKKK!!—*the chorus went on for a full minute or more.

An extra loud ruckus came from the coop one morning in mid-October. When I went out to see what all the clucking and cawing was about, I saw a miniature egg resting in one of the nesting boxes. My eyes grew wide and my breath caught as I lifted it, still warm, from the straw. This was the first egg from one of the younger birds. It was perfection—light brown in color and amazingly smooth, with a shape that fit in the palm of my hand just so. The little egg seemed to actually take on a translucent glow as I stared at it. I gently carried it inside and placed it in a bowl filled with tissues so it would be safe until the kids got home from school. The rest of the day had an effervescent quality; I felt buoyantly proud, as if the hen who laid this little miracle was my own daughter.

The remaining two younger birds touched my heart in turn when each laid her own small virgin egg, one even had a spot of blood on the shell. Creating and then giving birth to an egg every day or two must take an enormous amount of energy and I marveled at the care all the hens seemed to take with their purposeful work.

I also became intrigued by the ingenuity of the egg. They are very strong—many engineered structures borrow from their design—and yet they remain delicate enough for a chick to peck her way out when the time comes. Consequently, cooking and eating the eggs from our own hens became acts of reverence. I was acutely aware when cracking an egg open, noticing how orange and high the yolks were compared to the grocery store variety. We all noticed that the eggs had more flavor and there was no doubt in anyone's mind that they were better for us—we could literally *feel* the extra nutrition entering our bodies.

Once the younger hens got started, the eggs flowed freely. To answer a question I'm often asked: You'll never get chicks without a rooster, but you'll still get plenty of eggs. A sexually mature hen will lay an egg every day or so, just like a sexually mature woman will release an egg every month or so. A, ahem, *cock* is not required in either case.

This is just how nature works, whether we like it or not.

The more aware I became of the healthy goodness within our backyard eggs, the more conscious I was of all the bad news about food in general. It seems that so many foods are harmful to the planet, the animals, or our bodies. I felt powerless and frustrated. What was I supposed to do about it? Was the only responsible choice to crawl into a hole and die? Really?

I recalled what the woman had said to me in the consignment shop while I was still shaky from killing the rooster: *We're all here to serve one another. We take care of the animals and the animals nourish us.* It seemed to me from my experience, first with eating the rooster and now the eggs, that when we actually do take care of the animals with our own hands, when we pour our attention and love into them, then they nourish us more intimately than anything we could ever buy.

Over the next few weeks, this idea grew: Love is a nutrient.

As our family showered love upon our chickens, it was as if we were planting a vital element within them that expanded into something even more potent, eventually manifesting as an egg that gave love back to us even as we gazed upon it, but especially when we ate it thoughtfully and with intention.

We are nourished by love in more ways than we know. When love is present in the food we eat, we are blessed with ideal nutrition—it's exactly what we need every time. The presence or absence of love is just as relevant in vegetables as in the food that comes from animals. As I became more sensitive, I could feel the difference between spinach grown by a giant conglomerate in faraway California and the spinach I raised in my backyard. While food grown on a factory farm is often tainted in the rush to convert it into money, there is love in the leaves of spinach I grow myself or buy from a small local farm. Food grown in love will always nourish us more completely as each micronutrient it contains is more readily available to us.

I started shopping with this in mind, consciously seeking out organic and local farm-raised options, which often meant driving past the nearby chain supermarket to the Whole Foods store in Providence. It took creativity to be able to afford to feed a family of six like this, but when I started to shop with love in mind, I found ways. While I spent more money on high-quality, well-raised, nutritionally dense foods, I stopped buying lower quality foods entirely. No more breakfast cereals. No more chips. No more cookies. No more sodas. No more deli meats. No more mass-produced bread. Seriously, it's all crap.

The next time I went out to a restaurant, I ordered lamb. My research had shown that lamb usually has a better life than industrially raised pork, beef, or chicken. Still, as I waited for my order to arrive, I steadied myself, taking a long moment to feel the loss of the lamb that gave its life so that I could be nourished. Even if my loving hands had not raised it, I decided I would love it once it reached my plate.

After a lifetime of numbing myself out, it was not easy to bring awareness to such raw feelings and I almost cried, but as I finally bit into the lamb, I felt vibrantly alive. With every chew, I thought about the lamb—opening to perceptions about its life and honoring its contribution to mine. As I experienced all this more fully, I found myself wondering where consciousness began and ended. Perhaps the cells of the lamb still contained a certain sort of awareness. Perhaps it was "seeing" through my eyes for a moment, perhaps living *through* me as its cells became part of my body. I ate every bite with complete awareness of the lamb's spirit and with a joyous wonder at the possibility that it might be having the ride of its life.

Crazy? Maybe so, but loving the lamb and engaging with these playful thoughts was far healthier for me than eating without even noticing as most of us do.

As I became more conscious of food and its effect on the health of my whole system—physical, spiritual, mental, and emotional—I wanted to learn more about raising healthy food, which led to me obsessively searching the internet for farms for sale all over the country. I was absolutely fascinated with living the farming life even though I was firmly entrenched in my life in Bristol. What on earth was I thinking? With our complicated blended family and the children's other parents to consider, it was not possible to move more than 20 miles away. But I still spent hours online, often without blinking, looking at farms.

One day, I was drawn to a farm that was for sale in Upstate New York called Sweet Dream Mountain Farm. The website described the business the owners had built raising and selling grass-fed cattle for meat. I followed the links within the site to learn more. This was back in 2004 before I'd even heard of grass-fed meat, but I instantly felt the rightness of allowing grazing animals—ruminants such as goats, sheep, and cows—to live in harmony with their eons-old preference for grass. The concept is simple: An animal that was born to eat grass is healthy when it is allowed to eat grass. And yet, our mass-production food system forces many animals to eat lots of stuff that is definitely not grass.

My research helped me to understand why the general population in the United States was getting sicker and fatter. In just two or three generations, we've gone from raising most of our food ourselves or buying it from a local source to shipping it thousands of miles from the warehouses of huge agribusinesses. When you or I go to the store to buy a package of meat, we are not typically buying love. Most industrially raised chickens and turkeys are crammed into small spaces and spend their entire lives without being touched by a loving hand. While some grain-fed cattle are handled with care, more spend their final months standing in their own filth, eating an unnatural diet until they are fat enough to kill. Animals kept in this way are not only devoid of love, but they also are often sick, and the food we cull from their toxic and failing bodies makes us sick as well.

While this was all new information back then, there are now many documentaries that reveal shocking truths about our food supply. One truth is that while we have been told that meat is bad for us, the real truth is that, if eaten in moderation, only *bad* meat is bad for us. It's important to not lump the free-range chicken, pasture-raised pork, grass-fed beef, and wild venison together with the artificially pink, saline-filled, plastic-wrapped Value-Pak of hamburger we find at the nearby superstore.

Meat from healthy animals who have spent their lives grazing in properly managed pastures—especially animals raised in the presence of love and whose spirit is honored in their death—is among the most nutritionally dense food on the planet. When we commit to eating food that is nutritionally dense, we are satisfied with less, which is good for us and for Earth herself.

All of this research ignited a passion in me to be part of the grass-fed movement, so Paul, Mac, and I set off to see Sweet Dream Mountain Farm one day. This was quite irrational—I couldn't afford to buy the farm and there was no way we could move so far away, so why bother going? I wondered about that on the three-and-a-half-hour drive through the fiery oranges and reds of the late-October foliage.

When we finally pulled up the long driveway toward the house, I gazed at the pastures on either side, with two draft horses on the left and eight inquisitive black cows on the right. The real estate agent was there to meet us and show us around. Everything was perfect—the house, the barns, the land, the animals. Out in the pasture, we flirted with the cattle who looked out at us from under curly bangs and were alternately shy and interested. A black kitten wandered into the field at one point and we laughed as one of the cows pranced off after it.

I was absolutely enchanted. I wanted a farm just like that one and my brain was scheming how to get it before we even got back into the car. With Mac asleep in the back seat, I allowed the dream to percolate as I sat next to Paul on the long ride home. I stared out the window at the growing shadows and felt deeply content. But then something shook loose inside of me, interrupting my reverie. As I lingered over the possibility of creating my own version of the farm dream, it occurred to me that I didn't see Paul in the daydream.

This previously impossible thought would soon join other rumblings to create a seismic tremor that would rattle my whole world. Without my permission, the vision persisted—showing me a place where I would raise healthy, happy animals and where I would finish rearing a happy, healthy child. This would be a nourishing place where love would gush forth from the land itself. In the vision, I was a stronger, more vibrant person—a woman who would dare to use her voice to teach others about the importance of love as a nutrient and about other lessons not yet learned.

Part of me wanted to fly into this creative new life, but the bigger part of me wanted to play it safe. She was not yet ready to soar. In time, though, the farm dream took on a life of its own. It was a separate entity with no patience for the walls of the protective shell that prevented it from blooming into reality. It wanted to be born and its struggle to be free had begun.

LESSON 10:

LIVE LARGE

A couple of months after getting rid of all of our roosters, I ridiculously said Yes! to another one. Mac and I first met him on a bright but brisk November afternoon while doing our weekly chores at the farm. After first bringing some carrots to Blaze the horse out in the meadow, we scurried back to the old barn, eager for a break from the icy wind.

As we opened the corn bin to get food for the pigs, we noticed a little something moving on a rafter about four feet over our heads. We looked up to see a miniature gray rooster with comical feathery feet looking back at us. He was illuminated by a streak of late day sunlight that slanted in through the tall barn door. He cocked his head—first this way, then that—to check us out with both of his shiny black eyes. Then he fluffed his feathers, puffed his chest, and gave a big shake of his whole body. He was adorable in spite of all of his efforts to look tough. We spoke to him quietly, but he remained stoically silent and didn't even blink.

We scooped some corn into a pail and Mac led the way to the pigpen behind the barn. The pigs peeked over the fence at us with happy, mud-streaked faces. They squealed and snorted their excitement as they threw themselves against the wooden rails when we got closer, splattering mud over our boots. We carefully poured the corn into a wooden trough, which they immediately flipped with their strong snouts, apparently preferring to root around in the mud for their kernels. Eating is always such a party for pigs.

Mac carried the pail back to the barn while I cleaned and filled the pigs' water bucket, knowing that this was just another source of gleeful entertainment for them and would soon be tipped over to satisfy their eternal quest for mud. I stood and watched them eat for a while, delighting in their gusto.

When I returned to the barn, I found Mac and David gazing up at the little rooster.

"Who's that?" I asked.

"Well," David began before adding his distinctive pause. "That's a little Bantam rooster someone dropped off yesterday. Apparently, he got himself a bit stuck in the atrium of an office building in Providence where this person works. She didn't know where else to take him, so she brought him here."

I squinted with the effort of trying to understand how a rooster came to be stuck in an office building but then gave up. "How's he getting along?" I asked, choosing to focus on the present moment instead.

"Not so well. The other roosters pick on him, so he

spends most of his time in here. Bantams tend to like to sleep in the trees rather than in a coop anyway, so I'm hoping he finds a spot where he can be comfortable."

"Maybe he'd be happier at our house. He'd be the only rooster," I said matter-of-factly, as if I already was the confident fellow farmer I dreamed of being.

David regarded me thoughtfully for a long moment. "That might be worth a try," he said finally. I was grateful for his tact in not mentioning my recent struggle to get *rid* of roosters. The world needs more people like David who understand the value of the struggle and don't always try to save us from ourselves.

Mac rode home with the little rooster sitting peacefully on his lap. They fell in love and his name was Buddy before the car had even pulled into the driveway.

Buddy took up his role in our little flock with proud determination. The hens seemed to welcome him as their rooster, somehow aware of the natural order of things even though he was half their size. He'd make himself as big as he could and steer them around with a funny little sideways stepping motion. When the time was right, he even started mounting them and everyone seemed to have a good time, even though he was too small to get the job done properly. The hens didn't know any better and neither did he, so no one could be too disappointed.

Mac went out every morning to visit Buddy before school. One morning, I came back into the kitchen after my quick shower to see Buddy sitting on the kitchen island, sharing Mac's plate of scrambled eggs.

"Get that bird off the table!" I shrieked out of pure instinct.

"But look, Mom," Mac said, pointing at Buddy. "He likes the eggs."

I couldn't deny that he did indeed seem to like the eggs. Embracing my new attitude of Yes!, I whipped up another round of eggs and gave Buddy his own plate on the seat of the chair next to Mac. He stood on his fluffy feet and gobbled with gusto while he watched me with one eye, as if afraid I would change my mind.

After breakfast, we experimented with giving Buddy a ride on the dog. Shanti stood statue-still as we first let her smell the rooster and then put him on her back. She walked carefully, seeming quite proud of her new job as a chicken horse. Buddy wobbled as she moved, but held on for a while before fluttering to the floor.

After that, Buddy lived a double life. He had his important work as leader of the hens and his eclectic life as a house rooster. He ate eggs on the chair next to Mac before school and watched PBS cartoons from a towel on the coffee table afterward. He ruled the roost in both environments, even learning to boss the dog around.

This got me to thinking: If Buddy the tiny rooster could somehow get from wherever he came from to hanging out

in an office building in a city named Providence to ε
eggs and watching TV with a boy named Mac, then doesn't
it seem reasonable that any one of us humans is capable of
participating in even greater synchronicities and miracles?
So why do so many of us play small so much of the time?

We humans are complex beings consisting of emotional
energy, creative spiritual power, a finely tuned intellect,
and a sensory physical form. Unfortunately, the majority
of us use only a small fraction of our capacity. For most of
recorded history, Western culture has implored us to bow
down before the god of intellect and has only sanctioned
an awareness of what we can see and touch in the physical
world. Emotions have long been relegated to the sidelines
as something we need to get over quickly or bury deep.
And when it comes to spiritual matters, many are content
to remain in the dark. To be considered "normal" and "fit
in," most of us stick to this limited version of the human
experience.

The negative consequences of living in this way are
immense. By confining ourselves to only what we can figure out with our limited intellectual capacity and experience with our five senses, we miss out on a vast reservoir
of power and intelligence. I began to see that by repeatedly
making the choice to risk nothing and stay on the conven-
tional path, I had left behind the most important thing of
all: The Powerful Self I was Born to Be.

I had made the safe pick many times in my adult life—
staying too long in relationships that weren't right for me

and choosing boring work that didn't demand much. I also stuck to ideas that weren't controversial to avoid making other people uncomfortable. For example, when *The Celestine Prophecy* by James Redfield first came out, it lit me up. I became fascinated with auras and energy and tried to share the ideas with Paul. He didn't get it and he didn't want to try, so I put that book away and ignored others like it as I got back to "reality." It seemed scary to pursue topics that might cause me to outgrow him.

Living large meant that I would have to wake myself up—SNAP OUT OF IT!!—and kick off the chunk of my shell that had kept me pussyfooting around in my life. Maybe it was time to take responsibility for my own growth and happiness and free everyone else up to manage their own.

Buddy the rooster, on the other hand, was way ahead of me. He lived much larger than his little two-pound body would seem to allow. Somehow, he had strutted his way into my rooster-weary heart and taught me once again about the power of attitude:

We can each live as large as we choose to live.

LESSON 11:

FOLLOW YOUR SHIMMERS

The little gray rooster sat quite still on his perch up high on a rafter in the barn on that November afternoon as David climbed a ladder and reached out his hand. Buddy might have been afraid of this creature who was so much bigger than he was and he could have flown away, but instead he stepped onto the gentle hand, drawn toward love and kindness like a moth toward a porch light. Rather than retreat in fear from an unknown future he couldn't even imagine, he quietly trusted that the hand would carry him someplace good.

Over my time with the chickens, I can see how I too had opened to being guided by a benevolent hand as it tried to get me to notice the limiting aspects of my life and relationship. *"Look at this, sweetheart,"* it would whisper. Then, it would carry my gaze in another direction and softly urge, *"And now, Dear One, you must see this."*

But in spite of this gentle guidance, I had remained blissfully numb—choosing wine therapy over action and pleasantness over honesty. Yes, the flame had gone out on my love for Paul, but I was still carrying the candle around, hoping no one, including myself, would notice.

I had had many wake up calls in my life, including the dark days of 2001 that revealed the fissures in my marriage, but I had largely ignored them in my effort to return to "normal" as quickly as possible. Whereas Buddy had stepped onto the hand he'd been offered, I had scooted myself down to the other end of the beam, away from anything that might cause me to face changes that would rattle the status quo. Sitting safely up in the rafters of my life was just fine, thank you very much.

What made Buddy move toward the hand? I wondered then. Was it instinct? Or was it faith? What is faith anyway? Where does it come from? Where does it go when we lose it? What sort of vessel are we putting our faith *in* when we do manage to conjure some?

One definition of faith is to have a strong belief or trust in someone or something. To take something *on faith* means to believe it without question. This made it easy for me to see why a chicken might be better at having faith than I was, for I questioned *everything.*

What about instinct? People refer to instinct as a lowly function of the animal kingdom and far beneath us wise and conscious human beings, but it seems to serve the animals *so well* as they journey through the seasons of their lives. They somehow get a lot done without the benefit of a college education, a car, a debit card, grocery stores, or even a roof over their heads. They navigate through their mating rituals, raise their babies with care, find nourishment, establish territories, and do their best to stay out of harm's way. In addition to appreciating the good things in life more than we do (watch a deer family enjoy a new spring meadow sometime), animals also suffer their hardships with more grace. I believe this is because they never overthink things. They don't spin anxious stories about their future; they do not dwell on their suffering and misery; and they never compound the challenge before them by resisting and complaining. They just follow their natural guidance system and do what they need to do.

I decided I wanted a guidance system, too. I was vaguely aware of something inside of me that piped up now and then. How could I make it more frequent? How might I turn up the volume? Was it really that easy? Could I just listen and follow the instructions? How does one listen for such an ethereal thing anyway?

It would be years before I began to consistently practice and understand the benefits of meditation, but I had continued to try focusing my attention toward appreciating some detail within my present moment. When successful, this caused my clamoring thoughts to slow and a peaceful awareness to bloom inside. During those brief moments, I felt free—as if I were a little fish who'd broken through the surface of a murky pond to leap through the air and sunshine. I always quickly splashed back into my muddy everyday stress, of course, but in those moments when I could inhabit that lighter space, I was able to perceive things more clearly.

As I practiced this, I occasionally became aware of eloquent whispers, and I wanted to find the willingness to surrender to their call. Unfortunately, my ego mind usually protested, saying things like, "What is this 'surrender' crap!!!? Don't be an idiot! We DO NOT surrender to anything or anyone! We fight and we WIN!" But over time, I became evermore determined to override this incessant chatter.

Every tick of the clock was a fresh chance to choose to accept rather than judge, to allow rather than control, and to act from enlightened innocence rather than cynicism. Each time I chose to be in the light, I etched a fresh new groove in my neural pathways. By disciplining my mind and learning how to bend my ego to a higher will, I built new habits of thought and emotion that allowed me to slowly shift from being a recalcitrant and distracted brat in life's classroom to being an eager student who chooses to sit in the front row.

I paid rapt attention and did my homework, which consisted of acting on the guidance I received. The more I did so, the more frequent and clear the messages became. Whereas I had always thought of this phenomenon as a *voice*, it became much more.

As my habits of anxiety and control eased, I felt a wider range of emotions in my body that allowed me to become aware of a shimmer, similar to the way heat rises from the road on a hot day, except that it wasn't fully experienced as sight. More *felt* than seen, this shimmer goes beyond the visible spectrum to register as a particular vibration in my body—a feeling of subtle excitement, of eager anticipation. And just like the youthful vibration that had insisted I hatch that first batch of chicken eggs, when I felt this shimmer, I knew I was supposed to move toward it.

One dark, drizzly evening in late November, I received such a shimmer. While passing through Paul's office with a wide load of holiday decorations I'd just gathered from the basement, I bumped his office chair, which set off a chain reaction that would change my life. The chair bumped his desk, which jiggled the computer mouse, which woke up his computer, which lit up his screen, which revealed a horrid *beyond*-X-rated image. I stared at it, this problem I had been trying so hard to ignore, waiting for some combination of the desperate fear, hurt, and rage I had felt in the past. But instead, I felt nothing.

Nothing. I was empty space.

In the next instant, a wave of shimmery peace flowed into the emptiness—seemingly from above—and with it came a kernel of deep knowing that couldn't be denied. It was the knowledge that my marriage was over. It wasn't a question or an option before me; it was a complete and final fact.

I sat down in his chair, lost in wonder. The clear blissful peace was a new sensation and part of me was content to delight in it, but the message I had received was beyond imagining. After all of our years and all of our love and heartache, how could I be done with this man and this life we had made? My mind protested feebly, but my soul knew: Something greater than myself had made the decision that it was time for me to be free of the darkness and loneliness of his addiction. It could no longer be ignored. The message that flowed from the shimmering intelligence was simple and clear: *You're done.*

While I had been aware of the subtle wishes, I had never consciously considered actually *ending* the relationship; it would be too unbearable for us all. But here was this powerful knowledge that it was what I needed to do and with it came a calm assurance that the whole family would be cared for in ways I could not yet fathom.

I sat with the knowledge for the weekend, holding it quietly, waiting for the wave of panic that would certainly wash over me and remove my nerve. But it never came. I was steady in my resolve and the blessed peace never left, not even during the most difficult conversations or the times of greatest sadness. I had simply surrendered to a will beyond my own and trusted from the marrow of my bones that it would take us someplace good.

"I'm done" is what I said to Paul on that Monday evening, my voice calm yet firm. "I'm done with the darkness. I'm done with pretending we're happily married. I'm done with taking care of everything myself. I want to separate and, eventually, I want a divorce."

This was a shock to him—as it still was for me—but he did not have the blessing of knowing it was the right thing for us all, and he did not have the peace that goes beyond understanding in his heart. We each grieved in our own way, but his grief was mixed with an agonizing regret that he has expressed to me many times in the years since. He never laid his suffering upon me, though, as he could have. We always spoke to each other through the lens of appreciation for the good we had shared.

As far as the practicalities went, I told Paul we could continue to live in the house together if he wanted that. I saw no reason why we couldn't co-parent—we would both always love the children after all—I just couldn't lie to myself or him about our marriage anymore. My only stipulation was that he eliminate any possibility that one of the children would stumble upon an image such as I had seen. He agreed and sought help for his behavior, finally grasping the damage it had caused.

It was easy to separate our sleeping spaces as I requested—he had been spending most nights crashing on the futon in his office anyway. To his credit, he poured renewed energy into his neglected work so he could contribute more to the household finances. He also pitched in with the chores, showing up in ways that I had long ago given up asking him to. While all of his efforts made my life much easier and I appreciated them, my path remained steady. I was happy he was becoming a better man for himself and the children, but it was too late for us.

We told the children what was happening and of our intention to keep the household together for as long as we could do so in a healthy way. This conversation burns hot in my memory as one I truly wish I never had to have. They took it calmly on the outside, especially when we told them their day-to-day world didn't have to change right away, but what was happening on the inside to their young minds and hearts? I'm sure there is much I didn't do right—there is no manual for how to guide a child through heartbreak—but I had found the power to speak and live my truth and there was no going back. I could only hope that they might find good lessons in my example if they ever wished to look for them.

And so, shimmer by precious shimmer, I felt my way along during that holiday season of 2004 and, together, we all somehow made it into a new year.

Of course, such drama and deep thoughts were irrelevant to the chickens that winter. Already well-practiced in the art of following shimmers, they just went about their chicken business—enchanting us with their antics and sharing their genuine contentment while leaving strange dinosaur footprints in the snow.

LESSON 12:

LET GO

As winter's darkness finally ebbed, Paul announced his decision to move out at the end of the school year—saying it was too painful for him to live in the same house with me knowing there was no hope for us. Oh, God! This hurt beyond imagining! It shattered my stagnant illusion that we could just teeter along and keep things together until the children didn't need us anymore. But, of course, he was exactly right. Now that the truth had been unleashed, co-existing as we had been wasn't possible.

Unfortunately, even though I could see the greater good—I had initiated it after all—the actual physical separation delivered a staggeringly sharp blow. My heart stretched beyond its limits as new sensations of loss came crashing in. In addition to my own grief, I also felt for the tender young hearts in our home as we all faced learning how to live without the familiar container that had been our home and our life together.

In between the waves of grief, I saw that as I had clung to playing it safe over the years, I had stopped moving toward countless unknown blessings that had my name on them. This had had a constipating effect on every area of my life—from the material plane, to my emotional well-being, to my physical health. My basement, closets, and garage were so full of crap that there wasn't room for anything new in my house. My technical writing and consulting work at that time consisted of showing up at a university office in Providence and sitting around all day, being well-paid to wait for a project that never came. While I was very grateful for the easy money this brought to the household, it completely shut down all of my creative energy. Even though the chickens had taught me new ways of being, I often forgot to use them and found myself bored and lost in a foggy depression. Chronic sinus infections, weird rashes, and that pain between my shoulder blades were just a few of the ways my body protested my mental and emotional stagnation.

Letting go is an art and most of us mere mortals are not particularly good at it. Our lives should look like a ride down a flowing stream, one where we constantly let go of that which no longer serves us so we can enjoy the invigorating splash of our journey toward the new. Instead, many of us flail away, trying to beat the current at its own game by paddling hard upstream. Many more become content to live in the sluggish pools along the banks where the slime grows thick on the rocks, and aggravating little eddies keep us swirling amongst all the other detritus, going nowhere.

Some, like me, can get so comfortable resting there that we grab onto a branch to keep us steady.

It appears we'd rather be flailing hard toward an illusory goal or safely ensconced—even in an unpleasant familiar—than allow ourselves to flow freely toward an unknown. Yet the unknown is where our miracles live. Freely entering the current of life is our divine birthright. The ride itself is the *whole point*; there is no final destiny or destination. We can ride on, just flowing from one shimmer to the next until the end of time. We can do this alone or in the company of beloved others. The only thing that stops us is our forgetting that this is so. When we forget, we become afraid and contract, and that's when we let the eddies suck us in or start the futile paddling again.

Until we can dare to let ourselves be carried onward, we will never know the great abundance and joy that awaits us downstream. But first, we must learn to let go or, as was the case for me many times over the years, to have our fingers pried off the branch.

After Paul's announcement, the courage I needed to continue to flow onward had retreated. I had gone right back to hugging the familiar shore—swirling in a slimy back eddy and indulging in my old tonics of wine and mind-numbing television. My stubborn resistance to the flow of my life was not going to be tolerated anymore, however. Once the angels know we've learned something, we no longer get a free pass when we ignore it.

It was a cold clear day in late March and, for the third day in a row, my skull was threatening to burst. The angels apparently wanted my attention and hadn't been able to reach me through my wine and television fog, so they blessed me with an epic sinus infection that shut my whole head down. Any slight shift in elevation made my head throb from the change in atmospheric pressure. Two or three inches up or down and I was a goner, literally incapable of thought. I didn't want wine. Television hurt.

Determined to avoid antibiotics, I'd been drinking my fluids and using the neti pot, but all I really wanted to do was to sit perfectly still in the yellow overstuffed chair in the living room. Keeping my head motionless quieted it on the inside, too, which allowed my daydreams to rise to the surface. This was right where the angels wanted me. Unbound from the restrictions of my fearful and controlling ego mind, visions were free to flit playfully, like water bugs along the surface of my imagination. If I didn't move, it was actually a kind of high.

There were two days' worth of tissues all over the floor around the big yellow chair and I couldn't be bothered to pick them up. I had noticed that when I softened my gaze, I could pretend they were snow. Sweet Shanti was sprawled out on the couch across the room from me, a blur of black illuminated by a ray of sunshine that filtered in through the closed shutters. Given my addled state of mind, I didn't

confused.

question it when I saw another dog, a golden dog, lying on the floor beneath her. I also didn't question it when a knowing entered my mind that this imaginary dog was waiting for me at the dog pound at that very moment.

I sat there quietly knowing this until my bladder insisted that I get up to pee, forcing me to change my elevation. I blearily stopped to mention my vision to Paul as I walked past his office door, telling him matter-of-factly that a golden dog was waiting for me at the pound.

"I'm listening to you now when you say things like that," my newly estranged husband said to me. He did not say this in an effort to get me to change my mind about us; no, by this time he'd fully accepted that we were done. He said this because he'd seen firsthand how such guidance had graced my life during the months since I'd announced the end of our marriage.

After pronouncing his willingness to believe me, he pushed his chair back from his desk and followed me as I made my way to the bathroom off the kitchen.

"I'm going to the dog shelter right now to see," he said as he put on his coat and went out the door.

"Uh hummm," I muttered as I breathed through the pain of lowering myself onto the toilet seat.

By the time I'd staggered back to my chair again, I'd forgotten about the vision until my Nokia flip phone buzzed in my lap.

"There is a dog here that's just come up for adoption," Paul said. "She's a stray they brought in and the five-day waiting period to see if anyone would claim her ended at 10 o'clock this morning. She's the only dog here."

I felt something jigger in my heart, a subtle little dance step.

Then Paul added, "But she's not golden; she's black. Still, she seems like a great dog."

"Bring her home," I said, channeling a part of me that could still make decisions. "We'll see how she does with Shanti and the kids."

Within a half-hour, Paul had returned with a darling medium-sized mutt whose tail curved proudly over her back as she scampered into the living room. She was excited, her compact black body shaking with joy, as if she were returning home after a long absence rather than entering a new place. I reached a hand down and she licked it before running over to Shanti, who had hopped off the couch to get in on the fun. They greeted each other like old friends, forgoing the usual careful butt-sniffing of dogs who have just met. Paul watched all of this with me, both of us smiling for the first time in weeks. It felt so good to be truly happy together, even if just for a moment.

The dogs and Paul did a quick tour of the first floor. I stayed where I was, but heard the new one making herself at home by drinking from Shanti's water dish. Soon, Shanti hopped back up to her spot on the couch across from me and the new dog settled on the floor beneath her. I wouldn't have believed a dog could get comfortable in a new place so quickly.

After Paul went back to his office, I continued to sit

quietly, letting my beleaguered gaze fall upon the dogs. My earlier vision snapped back into focus. The new dog was indeed mostly black, except for her blonde lower legs and feet, which were the only parts of her I could see from where I sat—the rest of her body was obscured by the coffee table between us. I realized I hadn't actually seen the whole dog in my original vision, just four golden paws.

Tears sprang to my eyes and my head was too compromised to stop them, leaving a turbulent river of emotions to flow unimpeded. Somehow this little being had called to me from the pound. And in spite of any rational thought that the last thing on earth I needed right now was a new dog, here she was, clearly belonging to this broken family, this broken me. The feelings surged through me, joy mixing with sadness in perfect proportion, flooding dusty corners of my heart that hadn't seen any moisture in years.

I started to sob; I couldn't hold it in any longer. My grief over the pain I'd caused, over the losses of the past and future, poured out of my face from every orifice. Even my sinuses opened up and I had to grab the box of tissues to catch horrifying globs. I heard Paul come into the room. He stood politely to the side, an honoring presence rather than an intrusion.

"I'm so—" I blubbered, pausing to blow my nose, "so sorry for it all, Paul." I tossed the full tissue to the floor, where it landed with a satisfying plop. "We made this beautiful family and now it's over." I swiped my sleeve across my eyes and blew my nose again.

"I'm sorry, too," he said quietly. "It was my fault."

I covered my face with my hands and shook my head. "No, it takes two."

"I couldn't be who you needed me to be," he said. "I see that now."

A fresh batch of tears sprang up. I looked down and just let them fall into my lap. "Why couldn't I just love you as you are? I should have been able to do that."

"But you couldn't." He said it simply, without judgment.

"No, there was too much hidden darkness. It was killing me." I blew and dropped another tissue. "But this way might kill me too."

"No, you'll be okay now," he said from a strong and knowing place that made me think for the first time in a long time that he might be okay, too.

The new dog met Mac at the door when he came home from school that afternoon, bouncing up and down on her golden paws in an excited greeting as her curly tail wiggled back and forth over her back. I was feeling better and had left my spot on the yellow chair to watch. Again, I had the strange sense of it being a reunion instead of a first meeting. Mac was overjoyed and took her outside to meet the chickens. I watched from the window as the new dog sniffed at them through the fence. They were in the midst of putting themselves into their little shed for the night and her presence only made them go faster.

The rest of the kids approved of the addition, so she became part of our family as it seemed she was destined to be.

"What should we name her?" I asked as everyone gathered in the kitchen before school the next morning. She looked like a Misty to me, but I kept that to myself. Everyone agreed to think about it so we could choose a name when we came together that night.

Not surprisingly, each person had his or her own favorite when we gathered at the dinner table later. So after a spirited, yet inconclusive, discussion that included a contest to see which name the dog herself liked best, I threw out my pick.

"What if we called her Misty?"

This seemed to cause heads to cock and ears to prick up all around.

"I like it," said Katie.

"Me too!" said Patrick.

"Yup, that works," said Tom.

"Hey, Misty!" Mac called to the dog, who immediately ran over to him for some love.

"Looks like we have a winner!" said Paul.

And so Misty she became.

This is interesting because we later learned that this is what the volunteers at the animal shelter had been calling her during her time there. We did not know this. Not only did the shimmers guide me to the dog, they also guided me to her name.

After Paul moved out at the end of May, I got moving in every sense of the word. I felt compelled to be physically moving and I wanted to be completely *elsewhere* in every dimension—emotionally, spiritually, mentally, and geographically.

Therapeutic action began in earnest when I had a dumpster delivered. I hauled stuff up from the depths of the basement—three old lamps, a bedraggled futon, countless old cans of paint, an abandoned homemade puppet theater, an old chest of play dress-up clothes, and eight enormous engineering textbooks from college. The kitchen came next with its 27 jars of tired spices, dozens of cans of expired food, 14 old boxes of Kraft macaroni and cheese, a dozen cookbooks. Then I tore into the closets and found great piles of neglected clothing, costume jewelry, and a heap of unused toys. Everything went to a new home where it could be enjoyed or over the edge of the dumpster. I started to feel lighter with every load. Eventually, there was nothing left to toss. Corners were swept clean and empty space sat behind most closet doors.

Mental and emotional clarity returned as I shut the television off, canceled cable, and left the cork in the wine bottle. My spirit rewarded me with an ever-growing peace that transcended the transition that swirled around me. Throughout it all, Paul and I continued to engage as loving co-parents. I will be forever grateful for his ability to gracefully finish that important work with me.

Late one afternoon in early June, just as I was feeling a bit settled again, I saw a registered letter from the town in the pile of mail by the door. I felt a dread take hold as I opened it. I knew my taxes were current, so it could only mean one thing: It was time to say goodbye to my precious chickens.

Sure enough, word had spread to someone who didn't like chickens and the forbidding town ordinance was being invoked a full year after they hatched. Chickens, it seemed, could be kept in Bristol, but they needed to be at least 50 feet from a property line. My scrap of land was barely 50 feet across at its widest point.

I stared at the letter, poured a now rare glass of wine, and drummed my fingers on the countertop. My heart banged in my chest and threatened to tear me apart. I ferociously fought back against the pain of this newest loss and I even—in a blast of fervent indignation and outrage—quickly drew up a plan for a chicken house that sat on stilts 50 feet straight *up*.

I poured another glass of wine and mentally filled my hypothetical chicken skyscraper with noisy roosters who would crow loudly at all hours of the day and night from their lofty perch.

Grrrrrrrr. I was pissed. Who could I talk to? Who could I bribe? Who was the tattletale anyway? Where did they live so I could throw eggs at their house?

I spent that evening becoming powerfully unhinged by fanatical thoughts of wheedling, retribution, and revenge.

But there was, of course, no fighting city hall.

In the morning, I took three aspirin tablets to counteract the lingering effects of my wine and anger hangover and resigned myself to the fact that my chickens would have to go.

But I also knew—in my new and powerful way of knowing—that I would not be very far behind them. I simply could no longer imagine my life without chickens to care for, so my life would have to change in whatever ways were necessary for me to have them.

In that moment of acceptance, my farm dream became real. It bloomed in my mind fully formed. I saw not only chickens, but many other animals, too. And lots and lots of space and grass and air and light for us all to run around and play in. This was no longer something I *might* do someday, this *would* happen as soon as it could possibly be arranged. I did not know how this would all work out, only that it absolutely would.

My first call that morning was to David, who instantly agreed to take my entire flock at the farm where it all began. I was delighted. Our beloved birds would have more space to explore and a larger chicken family to celebrate their eggs with.

I shared the news with Mac later that day when he got back from visiting his dad. "Hey, buddy," I said. "I got a letter from the town saying we have to get rid of the chickens."

His little face fell. I hurried on with the rest. "But before you get too upset, tell me what you think of this idea: Let's go live on a farm of our own. Someplace where we can have lots of animals without getting in trouble for it. What do you think?"

I was rewarded with a huge grin, one with more teeth in it than when we had started this adventure. That night we took an early supper outside and ate with the chickens, dropping delicious morsels on the ground for them to enjoy.

"Can we get our chickens back when we have our farm?" Mac asked as the sun lowered and the birds started putting themselves to bed.

I had thought about this. "It might be a while before we can find the right farm for us. So I think it would be nicer for them to stay where they are with David and their new chicken friends at Coggeshall Farm. Why don't we get new chickens?"

His eyebrows furrowed for a moment. I thought he was preparing a rebuttal, but then he relaxed and nodded. "Yes, I think that would be okay."

It was agreed that Mac and I would drop the chickens off with David on that next Thursday afternoon when we went to do the chores.

We spent more time with them during those last days, letting every moment, every squawk, every egg, every dropped feather be a source of poignant joy. As I felt myself letting go of the chickens, the sting in my heart was balanced by a lovely sensation of flowing toward something even greater.

When Thursday arrived, we packed our six hens and little Buddy into three cardboard boxes and loaded them into the car. As we worked, I was filled with tears of gratitude for all they had taught me. I was a different person than I had been—softer, more vulnerable, more aware of the needs of my heart, more open to the flow of life. I had learned how to trust my soul to have its way with me, to say Yes! to what served me and No! to what did not. There were also tears of loss as the dear birds went into their boxes and we backed out of the driveway.

The sun was setting when we arrived at the farm. We had chosen a time when the resident chickens would already be tucked in for the night, so all the birds, new and old, would wake up together the next morning. David was there to meet us, steady as always in his acceptance of the natural way of things—sometimes things go and sometimes they come back again. That's just how it goes.

We carried the boxes from the car to the chicken house, moving in single file, regally even, like the three wise kings bearing gifts. David dragged over a hay bale for Mac to stand on so he could reach up high enough to help place the birds on the least populated roosting pole spanning the rafters. Then the three of us worked together to carefully place each bird up one at a time. There was more than a little commotion from the other chickens. They hooted and squawked and flapped, but nobody bothered to jump down off their roost. When we were done, we stood back and watched as our chickens followed their natural instinct to sleep now, wherever they were. Slowly, one-by-one, they each settled their fluffy bellies over their feet. Buddy was the last one to settle after clucking his messages of comfort to his girls.

"I'm glad we hatched those eggs, Mom," Mac said quietly.

"Me too, buddy." I said, welcoming a few more tears. "Me, too."

The chickens were content. And I felt certain that we would all be carried someplace good.

EPILOGUE

Within a year of saying goodbye to that first precious batch of chickens, I did find a blessed patch of land to call my own. It was a wild place without many modern comforts and that turned out—after many struggles—to suit us just fine. Eventually, my boy and I flourished there.

Living in a tiny cabin with no grid power or running water caused our definition of home to expand beyond the idea of four walls and a roof to include the entire environment around us. Since Nature does not bend to an individual's will the same way as, say, indoor plumbing or a light switch does, we were forced to surrender to her ways. We became much more aware of the cycles of the sun and moon, simply because we depended upon them for light. Water became precious because we had to lug it from the pond. We learned patience from the rhythms of the seasons, gained perspective from the enormity of the dark night sky, and became tempered by the extremes of weather. All of the natural creatures who lived around us became our teachers, too. After all, we never knew who we might meet on the way to the outhouse.

Our idea of family grew to include a bevy of beloved farm animals—there were chickens (of course!), plus sheep, turkeys, pigs, cats, dogs, goats, and a cow named Steve. We fed them all twice every single day and built fences to keep them safe. We delivered heavy buckets of water and cracked ice for them during the winter. We talked to them and they talked back, forcing us to find new ways of listening. We took care of them when they were sick and held a peaceful vigil when they died. We scratched them where they liked to be scratched. We loved them all.

We arranged matings and helped babies be born. Our hearts overflowed with joy when the births turned out well, and we bowed down before intense feelings of sadness when they did not. We also participated in the intentional killing of some of our beloved animals so the nutrition contained within their flesh could support our human bodies. Although we held everything about this taking of a life as sacred, and did everything we could to make it gentle, it never got any easier. That's because such an act was never meant to be taken lightly.

Misty, the little black mutt with the golden paws was by my side through it all. We worked together, often knowing each other's minds as we had from the beginning. She turned out to be a feisty defender who put herself in charge of watching over everything and everyone. Even me.

It would not be fair to romanticize this life as many do. There were days—sometimes months on end—when it felt like the inner gains I've described in this story had been lost. In those times of struggle, I often found that the Hoobly sun I'd rediscovered was too bright, and my life too large for the small, fearful person I felt myself to be. While those beloved chickens did indeed crack my shell, there were many moments when all I wanted was to shut my eyes and pull the broken pieces of my old normal life around me again.

But the natural way of things forbids this. Nature, who never wavers in her pursuit of creation, insists upon growth. Over the years, she prodded me with vibrant living examples from the wild all around me, and when that didn't work, she found less gentle ways to shake me free of my old shell. Eventually, I just surrendered and let her create me however she wished. The results have been nothing short of miraculous.

Looking back, I can see that my spiral upward toward a more graceful embrace of my own true nature had many twists and turns, but there was never a dead end, just as there are no dead ends in nature—where things are always moving, being recycled, and flowing onward to whatever comes next.

I'll keep writing and coaching and sharing what comes next for me with the hope that I can help a few more people kick off the shell that prevents them from living their best life. This work feels vital to me—I believe the future of the planet depends upon it. The reason we are in the mess we are in is that we have forgotten ourselves and fallen asleep in our modern lives. I invite you to join me in waking up and reclaiming yours. As you rise up to pursue your full potential, I will meet you there. Together, fully present and gloriously empowered, we can lift up the world.

ACKNOWLEDGMENTS

Writing is hard and its fruits are few. Therefore, I want to send love to those who have expressed support for my writing in general or for this book in its first form as *What I've Learned From Chickens*. Whether you know it or not, you have become part of my continuing journey as I've struggled to find my voice and my Self over the years. Some of you are dear friends; others sent me one encouraging note years ago. Thank you all for sharing your thoughts with me. You're part of the flock that helped me to finally leave my shell behind and fly.

Here you are — in no particular order:

Jill St. Claire

Kelly Jane August

Lisa Salinger

Jacki Mann

Marie Dumaine

Jet Tucker

Magner Peruto

David Ellis

Martha Sylvestre
Kendra Anderson
Christine Burych
Kim Steinfeld
Jackie Burleson
Linda Joy
Joan Solomon
Rob Emmons
Jeff Bella
Maggie Valla
Emily Spence
Josh Stockdale
Todd Winkler
Leslie Lindeman
Al Miranda
Cara Leonard
Dianne Heisler
Lee Ann Breeding
Rose Higgins
Janet Stark

Ceanne Richards
Tresa Salters
Dr. Pat Baccili
Alayne White
Cara Leonard
Katie Wygant
Kathy Piper
Paula Malady
Connie McGreavy
Denise Gadreau
Ktenia White
Sue-Ann Wayne
Debra Torris
Alberta Sequeira
Dianne Kelley
Deb Dwight
Donna Mac
Joyce Anderson
Pamela Kerouack-Warner

Thank you to my amazing editor Elise Macintosh whose wisdom and boldness has taught me so much. You are very good at what you do.

And an extra dose of love goes to my family — my mom, my boys, my beloved Peter. Thank you for being there through the scariest bits.

PLEASE REACH OUT

If you'd like to share your thoughts with me,
I'd love to hear from you. You can reach me at
sharon@masteryandme.com.

WANT MORE?

Visit www.masteryandme.com to find mindfulness and
meditation tips, occasional discussion groups, and other
offerings that can help you become a better You.

ABOUT THE AUTHOR

International Leadership Coach and Enneagram Teacher Sharon Wallen's journey has included many roles—from engineer to busy working mom to off grid farmer. Using the lessons learned from her first batch of chickens, she continues to embrace Nature's wisdom to create increasingly vibrant inner and outer experiences. She joyfully shares these lessons with coaching clients and audiences around the world. You'll find reflections, inspiration, and news about future books (including the sequel to Hatched) on Instagram (@sharons_path) and at www.masteryandme.com.

Made in the USA
Columbia, SC
09 September 2022

66855830R00088